second edition

# MUSIC
# IN THE
# MEDIEVAL WORLD

ALBERT SEAY

*The Colorado College*

PRENTICE-HALL, INC., ENGLEWOOD CLIFFS, NEW JERSEY

*Library of Congress Cataloging in Publication Data*

SEAY, ALBERT.
    Music in the medieval world.

    (Prentice-Hall history of music series)
    Includes bibliographies.
    1. Music—History and criticism—Medieval.  I. Title.
ML172.S4 1975      780'.902     74-23185
ISBN  0-13-608133-9
ISBN  0-13-608125-8 pbk.

PRENTICE-HALL

HISTORY OF MUSIC SERIES

H. WILEY HITCHCOCK, editor

TO LEO SCHRADE,
in memory of a great scholar and teacher

Printed in the United States of America

10  9  8  7  6  5  4  3

© 1975, 1965 by Prentice-Hall, Inc.
Englewood Cliffs, New Jersey

Cover photo: MEDIEVAL COURT MUSICIANS. Courtesy of The Bettmann Archive.

PRENTICE-HALL INTERNATIONAL, INC., *London*
PRENTICE-HALL OF AUSTRALIA, PTY, LTD., *Sydney*
PRENTICE-HALL OF CANADA, LTD., *Toronto*
PRENTICE-HALL OF INDIA PRIVATE LIMITED, *New Delhi*
PRENTICE-HALL OF JAPAN, INC., *Tokyo*

# CONTENTS

# FOREWORD

Students and informed amateurs of the history of music have long needed a series of books that are comprehensive, authoritative, and engagingly written. They have needed books written by specialists—but specialists interested in communicating vividly. The Prentice-Hall History of Music Series aims at filling these needs.

Six books in the series present a panoramic view of the history of Western music, divided among the major historical periods—Medieval, Renaissance, Baroque, Classic, Romantic, and Contemporary. The musical culture of the United States, viewed historically as an independent development within the larger western tradition, is discussed in another book, and forthcoming will be similar books on the music of Latin America and Russia. In yet another pair, the rich yet neglected folk and traditional music of both hemispheres is treated. Taken together, the eleven volumes of the series will be a distinctive and, we hope, distinguished contribution to the history of the music of the world's peoples. Each volume, moreover, may be read singly as a substantial account of the music of its period or area.

The authors of the series are scholars of national and international repute—musicologists, critics, and teachers of acknowledged stature in their respective fields of specialization. In their contributions to the Prentice-Hall History of Music Series their goal has been to present works of solid scholarship that are eminently readable, with significant insights into music as a part of the general intellectual and cultural life of man.

H. WILEY HITCHCOCK, *Editor*

# PREFACE

The historian of medieval music faces problems unlike those seen by historians dealing with any later periods. To begin with, not only are the concepts in back of the music of this time unfamiliar, but also the tonal results therefrom are strange to modern ears, results founded as they are upon philosophical and theological bases no longer current or common knowledge. Further, the difficulties of making medieval music easily available have been such that even those interested in the musical developments of the past in the larger sense have found it an almost impossible task to fit the two facets, the philosophical scheme and the practical productions, into a unified whole. Too often, historians of medieval music have spoken solely of the technical aspects of composition alone; too often, historians of medieval philosophy have overlooked the high place of music within the thought of the time.

It has been my hope that this introduction to the music of the Middle Ages will bridge something of this gap, tracing the interrelations between the labors of musicians on the practical side and the monuments of rational organization erected by the thinkers of the age. While the end-products, those compositions which have come down to us, are of importance as reflections of musical taste, their understanding and enjoyment can only be achieved to the fullest extent by a comprehension of all the reasons for the shape in which they exist, both technical and esthetic. Although much emphasis has been placed on the development of musical techniques, an equal stress has been laid on the forces, not always purely musical in the modern sense, that determine the path followed by the composer and performer.

In the ten years between the original publication of this book and the time of its revision, much work has been done by many scholars on the problems of medieval music. Whereas in 1965, the date of the first edition, there were but a handful of scholars, predominantly German, who were the experts in the field, in 1975 there is no such monopoly by any one nationality. The contributions made by American, British, and Australian musicologists have turned the exploration of medieval music into an international collaboration. With this goes the happy fact that courses in music history no longer skip over the many centuries of the Middle Ages as but a preface to the study of "real" music, that from the Renaissance on; the undergraduate today is almost as much aware of Leonin and Perotin as he is of Bach and Beethoven. It is a gratifying thought that this little book in its original form may have helped in motivating something of this change; the fact that a revision is needed and desired is flattering.

The changes made have been primarily in the direction of expansion. Nevertheless, the reader will notice that, with the kind help of H. Wiley Hitchcock, the General Editor of this series, many verbal infelicities have been eliminated and ambiguities straightened out; the book, hopefully, should now be easier to read. Many subjects not treated in the original edition are now discussed. There are many more examples than before, chosen to help the undergraduate in his first exposure to medieval music, to aid him in understanding better what he reads about it. All of this has been done as the result of conversations with many colleagues and students, not only my own at Colorado College but elsewhere as well. All of the bibliographies have been revised, with the goals of reevaluation and expansion; while not all the results of research done in the last ten years can be cited, I have attempted to include the most significant ones, particularly those which will lead the interested student into further independent exploration. Particular stress has been placed on the listing of modern editions of music discussed; it is here that the last ten years have shown the greatest production.

As revised, the book is still directed toward the undergraduate, one taking his first period course or his first survey. While it may be useful for the graduate student in one way or another, the book is directed toward an audience that is primarily of beginners in music history, not yet specialists, perhaps not even majors in music. I can only hope that the revisions will make it easier for these persons to develop a love and understanding of one of the great periods in the history of Western music.

I have already expressed my very real and deep appreciation for all the help given by H. Wiley Hitchcock. Without his comments and suggestions on all sorts of matters, the book would not be in its present form. Ms. Ellen Frerichs, a former student and presently secretary of the Colorado College Music Department, has spent long hours in putting the book into final form; she has also contributed many valuable suggestions for revision, based on her own experience with the volume as an undergraduate. My wife, Janine, has again managed to survive the experience; I can only be grateful for her comprehension of the problems and her encouragement to see the task completed.

A. S.

# INTRODUCTION

For the student interested in almost any human activity in that long period from the birth of Christ to the emergence of the modern world, that era we call the Middle Ages, its history is inevitably part of that of the Catholic Church. Beginning as a minor heretical sect within the Jewish faith, it steadily rose in following centuries to a place of supreme importance in Western Europe, eventually dominating nearly all phases of secular and sacred activity. With its objective the preparation of the human soul for a life to come after death, the Church early assumed the task of guiding life on earth in all its spiritual and physical aspects. Its preeminence began to wane only when men at last began to worry less about their future existence in heaven and to occupy themselves more with their present existence on earth. Its rise was a slow process, punctuated by the appearance of both religious and political leaders, men such as St. Augustine (354–430), Popes Leo I (440–461) and Gregory I (590–604), both given the appellation "Great" for their achieve-

1

ments, and Popes Nicholas I (858–867) and Gregory VII (1073–1085). The apogee of the Church's ascendancy came in the thirteenth century, the period of the final Crusades and the "political" Popes, from Innocent III (1198–1216) to Boniface VIII (1294–1303), the final Pope to claim that universal authority announced earlier by Gregory VII. It was this same century that saw the appearance of two of the great representatives of the Church's spiritual mission, St. Francis of Assisi (d. 1226) and St. Thomas Aquinas (d. 1274). After the Great Jubilee of 1300, the rising tide of secularization and national sentiment, the low state into which the Papacy rapidly fell, the Babylonian Captivity and the following Great Schism— all these and other factors combined to destroy a unity of Western civilization thirteen centuries in the making.

In view of the central position of the Church during the Middle Ages, it is no surprise that the primary function of music and musicians during this age was one of service to that institution. Although much music did exist for secular purposes and many musicians satisfied the needs of secular audiences, the Church and its musical opportunities remained the central preoccupation. No better evidence of this emphasis on the religious can be seen than in the relative scarcity of both information and primary source materials for secular music as compared to those for the sacred. Music in the day-by-day activities of European life always remained a favorite pastime, but little effort was made to preserve it, for, in view of the attitudes toward life on earth as a transitory thing, it could not be considered as more than a passing diversion, unworthy of special effort for preparation or preservation; the very techniques of preservation—by musical notation, for example—were not normally known by the secular musician. Only with the thirteenth century and after, when the previously accepted order began to change, was there a realization that secular music might be well deserving of the same artistic significance and meaning already developed for religious purposes.

Within the Church, music occupied a special place of importance, not only for its high position as a major constituent of the daily liturgical round but also for its unique role in the educational system of the time. As *musica practica*, it was a necessity in the various services of the day and, from the feeble beginnings of organized worship in the early days of the Church to the elaborate ceremonies of later centuries, the composer and performer found themselves required to lend their talents to the provision of music for a steadily expanding liturgy. This heavy reliance on the musician, however, cannot be explained solely on the basis that music provided a pleasant background to the services or that its place was the result of tradition and custom alone. Far more important for a realization of music's high position is the understanding of its other branch so important in the Middle Ages, *musica speculativa*, that area of music serving as a part of the long process of education needed for the philosopher and theologian. Here, the function of music was not one derived from its use as a sounding art but from its metaphysical possibilities, wherein it could act as a *speculum* or "mirror" of the universe, a means whereby one might comprehend the harmony of God's creations.

One may speak ideally of the relationship between these two areas of medieval music and their representatives as symbiotic, for the one could not have existed without the other; each grew by drawing upon the other for sustenance. The fact that music was defined as the knowledge of numbers related to sound goes far to point up the interdependence of the *cantor* and *musicus*, the terms used to distinguish the musician-performer from the musician-philosopher. Within the time it was the province of the one to provide the raw material for the other. As a theoretical science, music in its physical manifestations had to take into account the mathematical and metaphysical explanations and connotations brought to it by its place as a liberal art. There had always to be a constant recognition that technical advances by the *cantores* had, in the long run, to be related to the philosophical system as developed by the *speculatores*. The function of sounding music within theology could not be completely ignored by the practitioner. When considering music as a practical science, the philosopher was always well aware that the *cantor*, in his various technical innovations, had certain approaches that were of sufficient interest that adjustments would have to be made to include these new developments within the already established scheme. The medieval ideal was thus achievable only by coordination of the duple demands made by *cantor* and *musicus*, the first that music's sounding manifestations should have sufficient technical possibilities to intrigue the performer and composer, the second that the aural results should have the proper theological and philosophical foundations to allow for the appropriate metaphysical deductions.

It is evident that such a static relation could not endure, for the practical musician's interest in his own particular branch of music eventually led him into byways that were not always possible of easy adoption by the theorist. In the early part of the Middle Ages, few such problems existed, for the sheer size of the task of providing music for a steadily expanding liturgy gave little time or energy for anything else. However, with the passing of time, when the musical outlines of the services had been practically filled in, there was the artistic urge to extend and complicate what had previously been sufficient to fulfill the required function. In extending the place of music within the liturgy, additions were made to almost every part of the service, often without too much concern for the shape of the liturgy as a whole or without care for the overall balance of the various elements within it. It is no wonder that the

Council of Trent in the mid-sixteenth century found that one of its most
Herculean tasks was the pruning away of the many musical growths that
had thus been grafted upon the liturgy in preceding centuries, for the
musical elements added thereupon had, in many cases, almost completely
obscured the religious character of the service.

Until the thirteenth century, no problems arose to cause difficulties
for the theorist. As the accretions to the liturgy were stylistically no different from the material to which they were added, there was little necessity to take them into account. As monophonic works, the additions fell
easily into place. The first great crisis for medieval theory came with the
introduction and rise of polyphony, a technique of such obvious practical
worth that something had to be done. Quickly enough the system was
enlarged to accept the novelty, giving it a speculative justification that
encouraged further experimentation on the part of the composer. No
sooner had this difficulty been surmounted than the theorist was faced
with the recognition of advances in the area of rhythm, the development
of mensural techniques. As before, the theorist managed to find reasons of
speculative character that would make a new approach to rhythm part of
the philosophical corpus, although the task was not as easy as before. Up
to this point, the thirteenth century, the speculator managed to assimilate
the advances in technique made by the practitioner and to maintain his
domination of the situation.

With the decline of the Church's position and the rise of the
secular to a position of importance in the fourteenth century, the ability
of the philosopher to adjust himself to practical developments and to
adapt them to the system began to wane. Justification on theological
grounds for technical procedures became steadily less possible and the
composer began to work out his problems solely on the grounds of technical requirements, without regard for anything except the practical
solution of the problem at hand. No longer was it necessary that practical
procedures be reinforced by scholastic reasoning for acceptance; the
successful employment of technique or the offer of practical directions
was sufficient justification in itself. Although theoretical treatises in the
older manner continued to be written, expressing the traditional viewpoints of the past, inspection of their contents reveals that they were
completely out of touch with the practical events of their own day. Practical treatises, even though including many of the speculative elements
formerly so essential, no longer emphasized the relations between the
two areas; in most of them, it is obvious that, when philosophical excursions are made, the writer is making a bow to tradition before embarking
upon what is of real interest, the description of practical conventions. Up
to the thirteenth century, speculative music was a growing organism, expanding to include practical novelties as they arose; after, it remained

as it had been then, without change and with little power to influence or reflect the changed atmosphere.

Thus it is that our history of medieval music must mirror the alterations brought about through the continual urge of the practical musician to indulge an interest in his art as a technique and his obvious delight in the exploration of the purely tonal, with a consequent continuous overfulfillment of functional requirements. Beginning with the place of music in the Church, we shall describe this systematic expansion of the place of music within the liturgy, proceeding then to the growth of contrapuntal and mensural techniques as a new way of fulfilling those functions. With the decline of the Church's supremacy at the end of the thirteenth century, we shall note the broadening of the musicians' function to include the secular and a consequent rise of divergencies in musical practice between France and Italy. Finally, our story will close with the eclipse of those nations as the sources of musical leadership through the decadence of those techniques brought to their peak in the great era of Notre Dame de Paris and the introduction of new approaches from other parts of Europe. It is at this point that the music of the Middle Ages ceased to exist, for neither its speculative qualities nor its technical foundations were longer held as valid guides for new generations. The age of the Renaissance had begun.

## BIBLIOGRAPHICAL NOTES

The most extended history of medieval music in English is that by Gustave Reese, *Music in the Middle Ages* (New York: Norton, 1940); it is highly recommended, although it badly needs revision in the light of the discoveries made in the more than thirty years since its appearance. The most useful of the newer histories is Volume II of the *New Oxford History of Music* (London: Oxford University Press, 1954– ), of which five volumes have appeared. For a discussion of practical elements, Hugo Riemann's *History of Music Theory* as translated and edited by Raymond Haggh (Lincoln: University of Nebraska Press, 1962) is of value, although it does not go beyond the study of musical techniques.

For samples of the music, the *Historical Anthology of Music*, Vol. I, edited by Archibald T. Davison and Willi Apel (Cambridge: Harvard University Press, 1946), is indispensable. It may be supplemented by Arnold Schering, *Geschichte der Musik in Beispielen* (Leipzig: Breitkopf und Haertel, 1931). The opening section of Edward R. Lerner's *Study Scores of Musical Styles* (New York: McGraw-Hill, 1968) must also be mentioned, not only for its excellent choice of examples but also for its superlative notes. At the present time recordings are being made available for all material in the *Historical Anthology* through the Musical Heritage Society and the University of Southern Illinois.

Translations of excerpts from theorists of the period are given by Oliver Strunk, *Source Readings in Musical History* (New York: Norton, 1950); this is a major source. Other translations have been issued in growing number by the American Institute of Musicology, the Colorado College Music Press, and the Institute of Medieval Music. The principal Latin texts, although in need of revision, are found in Martin Gerbert's monumental *Scriptores ecclesiatici de musica*, 3 vols. (Typis San-Blasianis, 1784; many reprints), and C. E. H. Coussemaker's *Scriptorum de musica medii aevi nova series*, 4 vols. (Paris: Durand, 1864–1876; many reprints). Individual treatises have been published in modern critical editions by the American Institute of Musicology, whose goal is the eventual replacement and extension of the collections made by Gerbert and Coussemaker.

The interested student should also be aware of the excellent bibliographies in the journal, *Musica Disciplina*, from its inception in 1946 to the present. In addition, since 1966 there has been *RILM Abstracts*, which summarizes articles and books from all major musicological sources in the world; entries are classified by period. *RILM Abstracts* issues an unusually complete annual index.

# ONE

# MUSICAL AND
# PHILOSOPHICAL BACKGROUNDS

In view of the position of early Christianity as a sect within the long-established Jewish faith, it is no surprise that the foundation of Christian responses to the problems of liturgy and, by extension, the place of music within that liturgy were heavily conditioned by Jewish procedures. As Jews, the Apostles had been accustomed to a certain succession of liturgical acts; after their conversion, their major goal was not the construction of a completely new order of services but rather the addition of purely Christian elements to an already existing Jewish framework. As a sect within the Jewish faith, the first Christians spent most of their efforts on the conversion of their fellow Jews, utilizing the synagogues as areas for their preaching. Until the time of St. Paul, they continued to emphasize their relationship with Judaism, attending both the Temple (Acts 3:1; Luke 24:52–53) and the synagogue (Acts 9:20); even on those occasions when they met separately and solely as Christians, they occasionally referred to their gatherings as synagogues (James 2:2;

Heb. 10:25). In these meetings, they continued to adhere to the form of the Jewish service but with Christian additions. As in Jewish rites, music in the form of psalm-singing occupied an important place in the services of the first Christians.

## JEWISH MUSICAL PRACTICES

For the Jews, music had always held a major position in worship. As in many religions, music seems to have been considered as a kind of language peculiarly appropriate to communicate with God, for it was a manner of communication completely out of the ordinary interchange between human beings. Old Testament references to music as an accompaniment to the praise of God are many, from the accounts of special music on occasions of rejoicing (the "Song of Miriam") to the collection of psalms written by David and others. Within organized liturgy, the place of music was always high, for one special group of the Levites, the tribe of priests, was assigned the task of providing music for the Temple, the original center of the Jewish faith. Something of music's power and position in Jewish minds may be easily seen in a passage describing the dedication of the Temple by Solomon (II Chron. 5:12–14):

> . . . the Levites which were the singers, all of them of Asaph, of Heman, of Jeduthun, with their sons and brethren, . . . having cymbals and psalteries and harps, stood at the east end of the altar, and with them an hundred and twenty priests sounding with trumpets: It came even to pass, as the trumpeters and singers were as one, to make one sound to be heard in praising and thanking the Lord; and when they lifted up their voice with the trumpets and cymbals and instruments of music, and praised the Lord . . . that then the house was filled with a cloud . . . for the glory of the Lord had filled the house of God.

Although, in a large sense, the liturgical organization of the Temple services had little real effect on that of the Church, certain elements did exert some influence. Among them should be noted the establishment of the idea of a body of priests and musicians exclusively dedicated to their one task, with special schools for their training. In the ensuing centuries, a major part of the Church's work would be the founding of seminaries for the education of a non-laic priesthood and the provision of special choir schools for the making of professional singers. In addition, within the Temple services, certain psalms were linked to specific days of the week, thus suggesting a kind of liturgical organization; the Septuagint, the first Greek translation of the Old Testament, gives these psalms titles based on their place in the week's services. This feeling for ritual arrangement over a space of time was to be of great significance in the devising of a liturgical order by the Church.

More important for Christian liturgical procedures was the order of worship within the synagogues, the Jewish houses of prayer, praise, and religious instruction. Whatever the reasons for the rise of the synagogue, and there are many hypotheses, the fact remains that, to the average Jew of early Christian times, it was the focus of his religion, for every city and village with a Jewish population had at least one; some cities had several. For the Jew living outside Jerusalem and thus rarely able to attend the Temple, the synagogue was the place where he went to read, to pray, and to meditate. As the accustomed source of religious inspiration, it occupied a place in Jewish everyday life that the Temple, even before its final destruction by Titus in A.D. 70, had never occupied; with the definitive disappearance of the Temple, the synagogue became the center of Jewish religious observances. As such, it was that source of liturgy most known to early Christians and hence served as something of a model for their own practices.

Although we cannot be sure of all the details, it is certain that the synagogue services of the early Christian era were generally organized around readings from the Scriptures, a sermon, the singing of psalms, the saying of prayers, and the performance of songs of praise. In all of these except the sermon, music played an important role as the accompaniment to the word, for music had long been a traditional way to set apart the religious act and its texts from the everyday; the extraordinary nature of the service to God required extraordinary means.

Generally, there were two Scriptural readings, the first taken from the Pentateuch or the first five books of the Old Testament, the second from the Prophets. The readings from the Pentateuch do not seem to have been originally a constant part of the daily round, being reserved for the Sabbath (Saturday), Monday, Thursday, and special feast days. The material read was based on a liturgical division of the Pentateuch into short sections, insuring that the whole would be read twice in seven years. By the time of Jesus, readings from the Torah or the Law, the Jewish term for the first five books, seem to have become a daily part of the service. These readings were sung to a special set of formulae, indicated in later centuries by signs written above or below the words. Since the passing on of the tradition was done by oral and not written techniques, many different interpretations grew up in the course of years and we can know little for sure as to the specific manner used in the synagogue of early Christian times. The most important fact remains that Scriptural readings were not without music and that this music was based on the cantillation of standard formulae. The use of a specific liturgical arrangement of the readings is also not without interest, for the idea of a liturgical year is basic to Christian services.

Like the readings, the psalms sung in the synagogue followed formulae, but of different character because of their dissimilar function. In the psalms, unlike the readings, the congregation often took part, whereas the readings were reserved for one man. In most cases, the singing of psalms was guided by a leader, the *precentor*, a Levite specially gifted and trained. With the presence of the *precentor*, we see the use of certain performance practices, known as responsorial chants, which were later adopted by the Church. Of these, perhaps the most important is the procedure in which the *precentor* sang the psalm by half verses, the congregation repeating what was sung immediately after; this method was used for the teaching of psalms to children. A second method, used with the "Hallel" or "Alleluia" Psalms (Nos. 112 through 118 of the Latin Vulgate Bible), is that in which the *precentor* sings the first line, followed by a repetition by the congregation; the *precentor* then continues, with the congregation repeating the first part of the first line ("Alleluia") in the manner of a refrain. Finally, the *precentor* may sing the whole of each line, the congregation answering with the last half. In many situations even today, where trained singers or a professional choir is lacking, the same technique may be found. In America, these styles were used by the Puritans in New England and have survived in certain smaller churches to the present time, particularly in the South. A rather amusing description of the technique called "lining out" is given by Mark Twain in his *Tom Sawyer;* it is a direct descendant of Jewish practice.

In addition to these responsorial methods, there was also the possibility of direct performance, the entire psalm being sung by the *precentor* or the congregation without interruption. The choice of procedure in this case may well have depended on the nature of the music associated with the particular psalm, that is, whether it was of more or less difficult character. One other method is occasionally mentioned, an antiphonal procedure in which one-half of the congregation answered the other.

Unlike the readings and the psalms, whose formulae were primarily designed to act as ways of emphasizing the divisions of the textual line, the formulae used in the prayers and songs were of a more melodic character; they were used to impart something of the ecstatic feeling of the text and to suggest a more direct communication from the soul to God. Of particular importance for Christian purposes were the *shema*, a counterpart of the Credo in many ways, and the *kedushah*, a sanctification, much like the triple "Holy, Holy, Holy" of the later Sanctus.

In summary, the Church received from its Jewish ancestry a heritage that was to affect strongly the basic approach to its own liturgy. So far as organization is concerned, the major influence of the synagogue service was that of an overall sequence, a yearly round, with gradations between days of greater and lesser importance, the shape of the individual service being guided by the place of the particular day within the whole scheme. The use of Biblical readings and psalms as major constituents was also retained, together with certain other elements that fitted easily into the new purposes, the sermon as commentary and certain prayers and songs. On the purely musical side, it is evident that many of the formulae and melodies used by the Jews were preserved as a basis for Christian practice; many of the oldest chants of the Church have been compared with Jewish melodies, and the close connection of the two is clear. As a sample of the kind of similarities that can be observed, Example 1-1 gives comparisons of certain Jewish psalm tones and their later Roman counterparts.

**EXAMPLE 1-1.** From *New Oxford History of Music,* Vol. I (London: Oxford University Press, 1957). Used by permission.

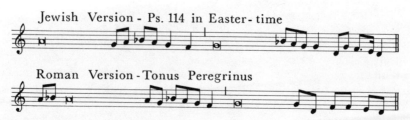

In addition, the methods used in performance—responsorial, direct, and antiphonal singing—became part of Christian practice. Finally, like the Jews of the synagogues, the Church in the main restricted the means to vocal music, for, like them, it felt an antipathy toward instrumental music because of the pagan connotations and worldly aura that went with this medium. Many early Church Fathers felt, as did many Jews, that God could be worshipped only through the human voice.

## EARLY CHRISTIAN ALTERATIONS

In making up one service peculiar to early Christianity, the fore-runner of that now known as the Mass (from "Ite, missa est," its last words), the principal change was the addition of a second portion to an essentially synagogue-derived first part, this latter portion being based upon the Eucharist or Lord's Supper. For the early Church, the Eucharist was the essential part of the Mass, reflecting as it did the spirit of thanksgiving over the giving of bread and wine; in later centuries, other and more far-reaching meanings were attached to its observation. The Eucharist was a part of the service in which specific commands of Christ were to be obeyed, thus a part that had no connections with the Jewish past; it was a purely Christian addition. Thus it is that the earliest services began with the remnants of the synagogue ritual, known as the Synaxis or Mass of the Catachumens (Learners); this was followed by the Eucharist or Mass of the Faithful. The first part was conceived as having an educational function and for this reason was open to all, including unbelievers. The second portion, that part peculiar to Christianity, was reserved for the faithful, the pagan and catachumen being excluded. While originally separate ceremonies, the first being carried on in the synagogue, the second in private homes, the combination of the two into one seems to have been fairly widely effected by the third and fourth centuries, with approximately the following scheme:

### Synaxis

1. A greeting chanted by the elder, responded to by the congregation.
2. The reading of three Scriptural passages in cantillation, separated by the singing of psalms in a responsorial manner. Originally, the first reading was taken from the Pentateuch and the second from the Prophets as before, but readings from the New Testament were gradually substituted for the latter. The third reading, a Christian addition to the Jewish original, was always from the New Testament. The choice of psalms depended on the content of these lessons.
3. The sermon or sermons, preached by certain priests and the bishop.
4. Dismissal of all those present who were not full-fledged Christians.

### Eucharist

1. Prayers of the faithful.
2. Offerings of various kinds placed on the altar, followed by prayers over the gifts by the clergy.
3. Communion, the breaking of the bread and the distribution of the bread and wine, followed by a psalm.
4. A final prayer and dismissal.

With the establishment of this broad outline, the systematic development of the liturgy proceeded rapidly, helped by the recognition of the Church in 313 (the Edict of Milan) by Constantine the Great (b. 288?–337) and his subsequent conversion. Under his reign, the Church came out of its enforced obscurity and began its first great period of church building, in itself an important factor in the regularizing and expanding of the basic pattern already determined. At this time, the congregation still took part in the psalm-singing during the service, with the psalms in the Synaxis performed responsorially, those in the Eucharist antiphonally. As the Church grew, however, the performance of music became more and more a province of the priesthood, particularly with the development of the *schola cantorum*, the singing schools that began to be established in the fourth century. Of particular importance in the encouragement and organization of music within that liturgy to become standard in the West was the work of Pope Leo the Great and Pope Gregory the Great, popularly supposed to have composed many of the chants later used; Gregory's role more accurately was that of codifier and collector. With the enlarged role of music, one may note an increasing difference in the music given to the trained soloist, of greater complexity and difficulty, and to the choir, usually simpler as befitting their lesser abilities.

By the fourth century the scheme of the Roman Mass, as we know it today, was fairly well stabilized except in matters of detail. No longer preoccupied by a question of overall format, musicians in the service of the Church turned to areas of elaboration and extension. In addition to recognizing the changed conditions of performances, i.e., the presence of professional singers, a constant effort was made to extend the liturgical organization throughout the year, with a goal of providing special forms and formulae for every day and every feast. On either side of Christmas and Easter, the two great feasts of the Church, extensions were made, to act as preparations and postludes. In addition, with the rapid growth of special feasts for certain occasions, for saints, etc., new musical requirements arose, for each day so added had to be differentiated not only by a specific liturgical content but by a more or less individual musical approach. The energies of musicians were almost completely occupied by this task for many centuries, for, although the organization of the full church year was nearly complete by the seventh and eighth centuries, the continuing process of sanctification and musical elaboration thereafter called for the creation of new liturgical and musical complements. Such a process of growth may be seen even today, for with each new saint a more or less individual ritual is provided.

In addition to the central ceremony of the Mass, certain other services known as the Hours or Offices developed in early centuries, generally built around readings and singing of psalms and hymns. Two of these, Lauds and Vespers, had their origins in the synagogue and corresponded roughly to the morning and afternoon services held there. A third, Matins, seems to have begun as a vigil in the night before special feasts, a meeting for prayers. Pliny the Younger (62–115?) mentions in one of his letters from around 111 that Christians in Bithynia and Pontus were accustomed to meet before daybreak on Sunday. Like the other services, these Vigils or Nocturns, as they came to be called from their time of observance, relied for much of their content on psalm-singing.

Further evolution of the Hours was a product of the monastic movement, particularly that found in the Near East after the third century; Alexandria seems to have been a particularly active center. While participation of the congregation in all the Hours was originally understood, this brought on many problems, as attested to by the many councils of the Church in the fifth and sixth centuries. With the promulgation of the Benedictine Rule of 529 and the establishment of the Benedictine monastery at Monte Cassino by St. Benedict of Nursia (480–543), the general place of the Hours became stabilized as monastic, and only Matins and Vespers were retained as services for the Church as a whole; it is for this reason that composers of later centuries concentrated upon those Offices for polyphonic settings.

By the sixth century, the day's services had been standardized as follows; this scheme has remained constant until the present:

| | |
|---|---|
| Matins (3 Nocturns) | During the night and its waning |
| Lauds | At cockcrow (3 A.M.) |
| Prime | 6 A.M |
| Terce | 9 A.M. |
| Mass | 10 A.M. (sometimes after Sext or None) |
| Sext | Noon |
| None | 3 P.M. |
| Vespers | 6 P.M. |
| Compline | At nightfall |

In conclusion, it must be emphasized that psalms were a constant component in all of these services, although of varying number and importance within particular ones. Herein lies some of the importance of the synagogue, for it was the source of psalmody, furnishing not only the texts but also the general procedures for their musical performance. Of greater moment was the Jewish assumption, accepted completely, that music was an integral part of liturgy, of such importance that it could not be dispensed with.

## THE PLACE OF MUSIC IN PHILOSOPHY

The high place of music in the Middle Ages, however, did not rest solely on its importance as a necessary part of liturgy, for music also held an essential position in the philosophy and theology of the period. Not only was it considered as the appropriate medium for addressing God, but it was also understood as a tool by which God and his works could be comprehended and interpreted. Music was thus unique among the arts, for it was an essential part of medieval education, in which its physical manifestations were utilized as the basis of metaphysical extensions.

Like the liturgy, the medieval system in which music played such an important role took centuries to develop, reaching its high point only in the twelfth and thirteenth centuries. Its early development was slow, principally because of the very nature of early Christianity and early Christians, as well as the social character of the world into which they came. Until the work of St. Paul, as we have already suggested, there was little attempt to spread the new faith outside Jewish circles; only after their missionary journeys did the early Christians realize that the world of the Gentile, the non-Jew, might bear more fruit. The pagan society thus approached, however, was not one of high culture or background; it was one in which the most appealing doctrine of the new faith was that of a world of bliss after death, a recompense for the sacrifices and hardships suffered on earth. Drawn from the lower strata, the new group of Christians cared little for the culture of their own society, for it was precisely this that they were attempting to escape by their conversion to the new faith. Thus it is that, in spite of the great achievements of both Greeks and Romans, including their highly developed philosophical systems, there was a natural suspicion of them that led, in the beginning at least, to an almost complete rejection of all that came from these tainted sources. Greek philosophy, Greek music, and their Roman derivations were filled with connotations that were abhorred by the simple men who spread early Christianity.

The rising importance of Christianity in succeeding centuries brought in a new class of converts, not always convinced so easily through an emotional appeal. Such men needed to be persuaded in terms of logic, to be provided reasonable accommodations with that which they already believed through their pagan past. Thus there steadily grew a need for understanding of pagan philosophy, either to refute those points not held by Christian beliefs or to reconcile those approaches held in common. By the fourth century, beginnings had been made at the assimilation of the Classic past, as can be seen in the works of such early Church Fathers as Clementine of Alexandria (150?–215?), Origen (184?–253) and Eusebius (265?–340?), men whose spheres of activity lay in the East.

In the West, the problem was not as simple. Although the universal character of the Roman Empire had made the spread of Christianity easy, its very size and concomitant vulnerability had brought on difficulties of a political and social nature that affected strongly the closeness of ties between East and West. Barbarian pressures from the North, continual economic crises, the failure of legitimacy as a principle in the choice of emperors, all led to a situation in which the now top-heavy Roman *imperium* was weakened to such a point that disintegration was a natural consequence. The most obvious sign of this breakdown was the separation of East and West into separate areas, a process begun under Diocletian in the third century as a purely administrative procedure, but made permanent at the death of Theodosius in 395. With this split, which affected all areas of human activity, the West lost almost all contact with the traditions of the East, including familiarity with Greek as a living language; henceforth, acquaintance with Greek philosophical achievements had to be made through Latin intermediaries. With the inroads of the barbarians and the consequent civil confusion, the only organism intent on preserving past cultural achievements was the Church, with monasteries playing the principal role by their seclusion from the world of war and ravagement; even these, however, could do little against the impact of the times of trouble that swept early medieval Europe.

By the seventh century, no Greek works were directly known to the West and pitifully few were available at all, and those that were available were Latin translations that often distorted rather than translated.

For Western music, the most important survival of the past was the Roman system of education of which music was a part. This curriculum, not completely described or codified until the time of Anicius Manlius Severinus Boethius (470?–525), was based upon a logical progression from the seven liberal arts as the foundation, followed by the intermediary stage of philosophy, and capped by theology. The basic approach from the liberal arts was divided into two levels, the first the *trivium* or *artes triviales,* i.e., grammar, rhetoric, and dialectic, and the second the *quadrivium* or *artes reales,* arithmetic, geometry, music, and astronomy. The term "liberal" as used here was taken to mean subjects either suitable for the education of a free man or studies designed to free him from the domination of the senses. Without passage through the *trivium* and *quadrivium,* no further progress was possible, for it was here that the foundations for the higher subjects were laid.

The ideas on the meaning of music within this framework were derived from those of Greek philosophers such as Pythagoras, Plato, and Aristotle, but none of them was at more than second- or third-hand, being transmitted always through intermediaries. Although the major source of attitudes was Plato, his views were not derived directly, but came principally through the commentary made on the *Timaeus* by Chalcidius (early fourth century) and the successors of Plato, the neo-Platonists, whose most important representative was Plotinus (204–269) and whose major Christian promulgator in the West was St. Augustine (354–430). Certain ideas of Pythagoras and his followers were echoed by Chalcidius, Martianus Capella (early fifth century), and Macrobius (fifth century). *The Marriage of Philology and Mercury* by Martianus Capella, written between 410 and 439, while of little immediate impact on Boethius, was constantly referred to in the time of Charlemagne and after and was used as a textbook by many of the Irish scholars who migrated to France and its surrounding areas in the ninth century. Certainly his division of the liberal arts into the two stages of *trivium* and *quadrivium* remained central to medieval education, with the essay on music (Book IX of the *Marriage*) of particular influence on such later writers as Johannes Scotus Erigena and Remigius of Auxerre, both of the ninth century. Macrobius is most important for his *Commentary on the "Dream of Scipio,"* the closing portion of the sixth book of Cicero's long essay, *De re publica.* Cicero's original is quite short and is primarily a study of *musica mundana.* In his commentary, Macrobius amplifies the proportional and mathematical foundations behind Cicero's more general statements; his book became part of the basic library of the medieval writer on music and

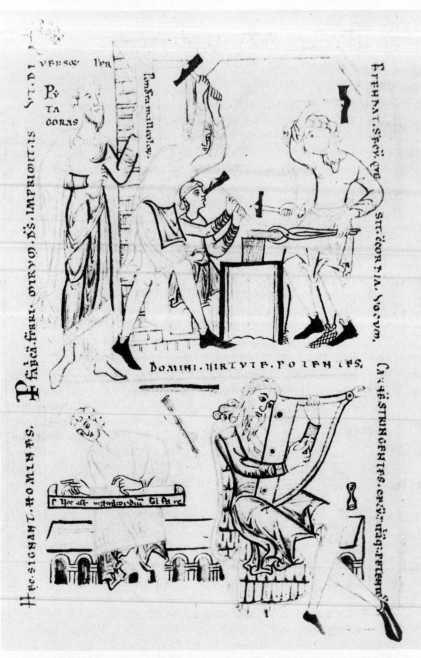

Munich, Staatsbibliothek, Lat. 2599, folio 96 verso. At the top is Pythagoras, listening to the sound of the hammers, from which he derived the proportions for the octave, perfect fifth, perfect fourth, and whole tone (see p. 19). At the lower right is King David, playing on his harp. At the lower left, Guido of Arezzo is depicted, working out tonal proportions on the monochord, that one-stringed instrument which demonstrated the mathematics of music in sound.

was borrowed from and referred to by most authors as one of the great authorities. He is, in the minds of many scholars, a major source of neo-Platonism in the West.

Although all the men mentioned above are important as sources for the role of music in medieval philosophy, the outstanding figure is Boethius, for it was his early incomplete treatise, the *De Musica*, that furnished most of the foundation for later ages; although the names of many writers are found scattered through the treatises of later times, it is always clear that the essential source is Boethius and that it is his doctrines which dominate.

## THE PHILOSOPHY OF BOETHIUS

In essence, Boethius's work is an attempt to include Pythagorean elements within a reconciliation of neo-Platonic and Aristotelian elements. While following the same neo-Platonism as that of St. Augustine in many ways, he was heavily influenced by the many commentaries on and translations of Aristotle that he himself had done. In *De Musica*, his philosophical approach to music is generally neo-Platonic with admixtures of the Pythagorean, while his placing of it within the educational scheme is Aristotelian.

At the root of Boethius's ideas is the concept that music is number made audible. This is illustrated by a legend of Pythagoras, echoed by later writers. It seems that Pythagoras was wandering one day in the forest and, passing by a forge, heard such wonderful harmonies from four hammers beating on anvils that he stopped to investigate. Determining that the sounds were caused by the heads of the hammers, he then weighed them, discovering that their weights were, respectively, 12, 9, 8, and 6 pounds. The sound of the octave was given by the relation of the 12-pound hammer to that of the 6, or 2:1; the perfect fifth resulted from the comparison of that of 12 and that of 8, or of those of 9 and 6, or 3:2; the perfect fourth from that of the 8 and 6, or 12 and 9, 4:3; and the whole tone from that of 9 and 8. That these sounds were harmonious is explained, according to Pythagoras and his followers, by their numerical ratio, for the simpler the numerical relationship, the more beautiful is the sound. Music demonstrates in sound the pure world of number and derives its beauty from that world.

It is not just music, however, that is beautiful because of its dependence on number, but everything. Hence, all things that are beautiful are subject to the power of number and can be explained by it. The most beautiful thing is God, and the world is but a reflection of God's beauty, just as man's beauty is a reflection of that of the world. All of these beauties may then be expressed as forms of numerical ratio, ratio that has been made easily sensed by the ear in music. Thus it is that music stands as a way of depicting the beauty and perfection of God and his creations, the world and man. It is here that music achieves its real place in medieval philosophy, for as a microcosm in the macrocosm it can duplicate on a small scale the power of number inherent in the otherwise almost incomprehensible grand expanse about us.

To carry out the implications of this position, Boethius divided music into three levels, *musica instrumentalis, musica humana,* and *musica mundana,* three divisions that were to remain immutable for the remainder of the age with but one change, that of *musica mundana* to *musica caelestis. Musica instrumentalis,* at the lowest level, is that music which is sounding, both vocal and instrumental. Its primary purpose is the concrete demonstration of the fundamental ratios, a demonstration made clear by the use of a one-stringed instrument, the monochord, on which the ratios could be measured off in physical distances. Those intervals whose ratios were simplest—the octave, perfect fifth, and perfect fourth—were labeled as consonances, all others as dissonances.

On the second level, Boethius placed *musica humana,* "*humana*" being interpreted both physically and spiritually. In the first sense, reference is made to the external symmetry of the human body, the balance of its members and their placement; in addition, there is the beauty of the internal organs and their arrangement, as well as the harmony between their functioning and man's well-being. On the other hand, there is also a harmonious relation between the body and the soul, a harmony seen in the health of the body and the functions of the soul—intelligence, love, etc. These relationships are a form of music, for they are, like music, founded on the same numerical laws.

The highest level, that of *musica mundana* or, as it is usually called, "the music of the spheres," is that harmony standing as the foundation of all the world about us, not only that on earth but also that of the stars and planets, as well as heaven itself. It is the regular succession of the seasons, the months, and years; the movements of the heavens; the varying combinations of the four elements (fire, earth, air, and water); and, as a purely Christian addition to Boethius's original definition, the music heard around the throne of God, when the angels sing, "Holy, Holy, Holy." Again, like *musica humana, musica mundana* has proportion as a governor and therefore is subject to interpretation as music. The movement of the planets was thought by many medieval philosophers to produce sound, a true "music of the spheres"; that this sound was unheard was because of a lack of sensitivity in men's ears. Others argued that sound was not a part of *musica mundana* by its very nature.

With this scheme in mind, it is easy to understand the medieval definitions of various kinds of musicians, for specific terms were used to indicate specific levels. It was not enough to produce or enjoy music as an aural delight; the men who did only this, the *cantores*, knew only the how. The true *musicus* was one who knew the why, the ratios in back of the delight that he obtained; to use Boethius's words, "the musician is he to whom belongs the ability to judge." This clear distinction is fundamental to an understanding of the relative places of the practitioner and theorist, for it explains the high place given to what we would today call a critic and indicates the necessity that the practical manifestations of music be capable of philosophic explanation; *musica instrumentalis* as the lowest of the three levels had to be subject to the speculative insight derived from the other two, all based on the law of number.

The Boethian scheme of levels of kinds of music was not the only one to appear in the treatises of medieval writers, for the definition of music and its areas assumed many shapes during the period. Nevertheless, there is a certain similarity between all of them because there is at the top of the hierarchy a kind of music that is celestial and at the bottom there is the purely sounding music which is the product of human activity. As one example, we may cite the approach of Johannes Scotus Erigena (810–886), in part derived from Martianus Capella. He speaks of but two broad categories of music, *musica naturalis* and *musica artificialis*. Natural music is that which is not made by instruments or by man; it comes from the divine, i.e., it includes the music of the spheres, the harmony of the body and the soul. Here, it is analogous to Boethius's *musica mundana* and *musica humana*, described above. The second category, artificial music, is that created by man, a manifestation in tangible sound of that which is intangible in the higher classification, natural music. One must begin with that which can be sensed, the corporeal or artificial, in order to gain a comprehension of that which cannot, the divine or natural.

In general terms, this duple classification is quite similar to the triple one made by Boethius. But Erigena and his followers, Remigius of Auxerre (841?–908?) and Regino of Prüm (860?–915), added the qualification that this natural music was sung to the eight tones of ecclesiastical music, the eight modes used as a way of ordering plainchant. As stated by Calvin M. Bower in an excellent article, "Natural and Artificial Music: The Origins and Development of an Aesthetic Concept" (*Musica Disciplina*, 1971), "The first principle of natural music was the tone, the mode; and all music developed from and according to this principle and ultimately returned to it. The modes were present in music sung to the praise of God, and music sung in divine praise on earth was a reflection of the divine praises eternally sung in the celestial realm." This idea that the manner in which the church classified its practical musical expressions in the same manner as the music of God lent great weight to the pronouncements made on music by ecclesiastical authorities speaking in the name of God. One may see here another reinforcement of the authority of the theorist as a judge and as a guide for the practical musician. Again, theological and philosophical justification of practical achievements remained paramount.

Writing on music was thus obviously divided into two broad areas, the first theoretical or speculative, the second practical. This division is clearly reflected in the works of later writers, for each author normally had quite clearly in mind the particular audience to whom his remarks were addressed. The treatise prepared for the student of philosophy and usually known as the *protreptikos* is primarily hortatory, encouraging the student by showing him the necessity of musical study through its classifications and relations to other arts; Boethius's *De Musica* is itself an example. Shorter versions specifically referring to music's place in philosophy might be inserted into broader treatises; the sections on music found in larger works by Roger Bacon and St. Thomas Aquinas are cases in point. Finally, there is the direct introduction to the subject (*eisagogé*), organized in a set pattern of topics or *kephalaia*, exploring the field more deeply through definitions, classification, and exploration of the number relationships; the tenth-century *De harmonica institutione* by Regino of Prüm falls into this category.

Like the speculative treatises, the practical ones are also divided by audience, for their complexity may vary greatly in accord with the needs of the reader. At the simplest level, there are works directed toward the singer and designed to help him solve the practical problems arising from his function within the liturgy. Some give little more than simple prescriptions for the performance of plainchant, with aids to the correct ordering of the modes and the chants within each mode; as the complexity of music increased, these treatises expanded to the teaching of notation, of polyphony, of rhythm and related subjects. In all of these, little attention is paid to philosophical meaning, for speculative excursions have nothing to do with the main goal, the correct performance of music in liturgy. This type is exemplified in the several treatises of Guido of Arezzo (995?–1050), who remarks at one point that he is omitting many things useful to the philosopher but of little moment for the singer.

Certain philosophic points do occur in some practical treatises, the *kephalaia* mentioned earlier, for a learned audience might well feel such topics of value. In these, the philosophical meanings are used to support practical procedures, with speculative elements as a rational background. Many of these works are quite large, for they attempt to encompass all knowledge of the field, producing in music a *speculum* much as the same type of treatise did in theology. The somewhat shorter type is best seen in the thirteenth-century compilation of many treatises made by Jerome of Moravia, the *Tractatus de Musica*, while the longer encyclopedic approach may be found in the *Speculum musicae* by Jacques de Liège, of the early fourteenth cenutry.

## BIBLIOGRAPHICAL NOTES

Of particular value for the early musical and liturgical relations between the Jewish and Christian faiths is Eric Werner's *The Sacred Bridge* (New York: Columbia University Press, 1956), together with his articles in various issues of the *Hebrew Union College Annual*. Many other items of interest are listed in A. Sendrey's extensive *Bibliography of Jewish Music* (New York: Columbia University Press, 1951); special emphasis must be laid on the extensive contributions of Abraham Z. Idelsohn.

For the development of Christian liturgy, Adrien Fortescue's *The Mass* (London: Longmans, 1912) and *The Early Liturgy* by Josef A. Jungmann (Notre Dame: University of Notre Dame Press, 1959) are fundamental, although they say little about the music. For this facet, see Willi Apel, *Gregorian Chant* (Bloomington: Indiana University Press, 1958). Useful information is also given in the articles by Egon Wellesz and Higini Anglés in Vol. II of the *New Oxford History of Music* (London: Oxford University Press, 1954).

The major study on the meaning of music in the Middle Ages is Edgar de Bruyne, *Esthetics of the Middle Ages,* transl. by Eileen B. Hennessy (New York: F. Ungar, 1969). For the Greek background, see Warren D. Anderson, *Ethos and Education in Greek Music* (Cambridge: Harvard University Press, 1966) and Edward A. Lippman, *Musical Thought in Ancient Greece* (New York: Columbia University Press, 1964). For a general background, Julius Portnoy's *The Philosopher and Music* (New York: Humanities Press, 1954) is of use, although his remarks on Boethius must be supplemented by Leo Schrade's "Music in the Philosophy of Boethius," in the *Musical Quarterly*, XXXIII (1947). The *De Musica* is still without translation; the latest edition of the Latin text is from 1871 (Lipsiae: Teubner) and more than ever needs revision. For Macrobius, the *Commentary on the "Dream of Scipio"* has been beautifully translated and annotated by William H. Stahl (New York: Columbia University Press, 1966); the same author has also published a study, *Martianus Capella and the Seven Liberal Arts* (New York: Columbia University Press, 1971), which is equally recommended.

For general viewpoints on medieval civilization, the handiest compendium is that of R. W. Southern, *Medieval Humanism* (New York:

Harper, 1970); of great value also is Henry O. Taylor's two-volume *The Medieval Mind* (Cambridge: Harvard University Press, 1949), with help from the first volume of Maurice deWulf's *History of Medieval Philosophy* (New York: Dover, 1952). Nan Cooke Carpenter gives much information on the types of medieval music treatises and their place in education in her *Music in Medieval and Renaissance Universities* (Norman: University of Oklahoma Press, 1958).

# TWO

# PLAINCHANT

The previous chapter has pointed out that it was only by the third and fourth centuries that a somewhat standard liturgical pattern was achieved by the Christian Church. In spite of general agreement on the outline, many local variations around the central theme continued to develop, primarily because of a lack of communication between one area and another, the autonomy of local bishops, and the growth of individual traditions. Music of the liturgy likewise showed a lack of unity, not only for the above reasons but because of the inability to preserve a specific melody unchanged; oral tradition could not prevent alterations over many generations. The final stabilization of plainchant into fixed melodies came only later, with the growth of more or less precise notational techniques. As a result of all these factors, the fourth through the sixth centuries saw the rise of many differing liturgical forms in various

areas, all observing the same general plan but with individual characteristics in details of both rites and music.

   With increasing unification of the Church under the Bishop of Rome
and the latter's eventual assumption of the role of Western spiritual
leadership, steady attempts were made to eradicate divergencies in liturgical practice, the goal being conformity to Roman procedures. Nat-
urally, opposition was great and the process of standardization was slow,
but by the eleventh century the task was accomplished. Certain variations
continued to exist here and there in choices of texts and in the music, but
not in the basic outline; and even these variations disappeared with the
Council of Trent in the sixteenth century. Since we cannot explore in
detail all the various manners of liturgy, it seems best to restrict our discussion to that of Rome; some mention of the others will be made at the
end of this chapter.

## ROMAN LITURGY—THE MASS

The organization of the liturgical year is founded on two types of
feast, represented by the two great events of Christ's life, the Nativity
and Easter. The first type, the fixed feast, is one whose place is set upon
a specific date such as Christmas, which always falls on December 25.
The second is the moveable feast; its date is set by its relation to Easter,
also moveable. The year begins with Advent, a preparation for Christmas,
moves through the Christmas season, and proceeds to Septuagesima
Sunday, itself beginning the pre-Easter period. With Ascension Sunday
as a close to Easter, the prelude to Pentecost and its associated feasts is
begun, with a transition to Advent at their end.

   As the major service of each day, the Mass reflects the character
of that day by utilizing, in addition to constant elements whose text is
unvarying (the Ordinary), certain others whose functions are unchanging
but whose texts vary according to the day (the Proper). Within each
category some items are intoned to formulae, others to specific melodies;
it is this latter group of chants that is of primary importance to the history
of music, for it was within them that the talents of performer and composer found their fullest expression. So that comparison may be made
between the final plan and the earlier outline as given in the preceding
chapter, a listing of all parts of the Roman Mass follows here, indicating
the place of each portion as Proper (P) or Ordinary (O) and showing
whether sung (S) or intoned (I):

| [*Synaxis*] | [*Eucharist*] |
|---|---|
| Introit (PS) | Preface (PI) |
| Kyrie (OS) | Sanctus (OS) |
| Gloria (OS) | Canon (OI) |
| Collect (PI) | Agnus Dei (OS) |
| Epistle (PI) | Communion (PS) |
| Gradual (PS) | Post-Communion (PI) |
| Alleluia *or* Tract (PS) | Ite missa est *or* Benedicamus Domino (OS) |
| Evangelium (PI) | |
| Credo (OS) | |
| Offertory (PS) | |
| Secret (PI) | |

It will be noted that the earlier division between the two parts of the Mass is no longer in exactly the same place; this seems to have come about in part through the loss of the teaching function of the Synaxis. All attending Mass were now Christians.

In view of the specific nature of the Proper chants, their place within the liturgy is higher than that of the Ordinaries; indeed, the latter entered the Mass at a later period and even now are not as necessary, for the Gloria and Credo are omitted in certain seasons. The two categories also differ in their musical character, for the Proper chants, designed originally for a trained choir or schooled soloists, are more elaborate than those of the Ordinary, which were intended in the beginning for the congregation or officiating clergy; with the taking over of the Ordinary chants by the choir this difference gradually became less obvious. Finally, the texts of the Proper are normally Biblical, most of them being based on the Psalms, while those of the Ordinary lie outside that source.

Early performance of the Proper divided its chants into two types, those sung antiphonally—Introit, Offertory, and Communion—and those sung responsorially—Gradual and Alleluia. Of these, the Introit (its name deriving from its function as an opening) is today nearest to its original manner; its form is now that of an opening antiphon, a Psalm verse, the Gloria Patri (Lesser Doxology), and a repetition of the antiphon. In earlier times, the antiphon acted as a refrain between many Psalm verses, one half of the choir replying to the other half; today only one Psalm verse remains and the antiphon has been reduced to a frame for it. As with the other antiphonal chants, performance today is responsorial, the choir replying to one or more cantors. In the Offertory and Communion, the only remnant is the antiphon that originally introduced the Psalm; all the verses have been dropped.

As a responsorial chant, with alternation between a trained soloist and the choir, the Gradual (its name deriving from the steps where it was performed, the *gradus*) is musically more elaborate, although, like the antiphonal chants, it has been much curtailed from its earliest forms. Today, the opening respond is begun by the soloist and concluded by the choir; the following Psalm verse is similarly divided. At the end, there is a return to the opening respond, sung as before. The Alleluia is performed in much the same manner, except that in the opening respond the choir does not pick up only the last part (the *jubilus* on -ia) but repeats from the beginning. In both of these, there were originally many Psalm verses, but today only one remains.

During liturgical periods of mourning, the Alleluia is replaced by the Tract, one of the last remnants of direct psalmody left in the service. It normally contains three or four Psalm verses, although some may be much longer, as in *Qui habitat* (for the First Sunday of Lent), which includes all of Psalm 90. In view of its character, it has less musical individuality than the other chants mentioned, for it is restricted to a number of formulae, used in various combinations; it utilizes only two of the eight modes, Modes II and VIII (to be discussed presently).

Although the texts of the various Ordinaries are invariable, the effort to differentiate betwen feasts of varying importance has led to an organization much like that of the Propers, whereby certain Ordinary chants are indicated as of particular suitability for certain occasions. Five parts of the Ordinary, the Kyrie, Gloria, Sanctus, Agnus Dei, and Ite missa est or Benedicamus, appear in present-day chant books in eighteen organized groups (Masses I-XVIII), each labeled with its particular affinity, i.e., Paschal (Easter) Time, Solemn Feasts, Feasts of the Blessed Virgin, etc. In addition, there are "ad libitum" chants for each section so that, by making substitutions and variations, the needs of a particular occasion may be met. The Credo, because of its late appearance and lack of fixed place in the liturgy, is not part of these groupings. The six chants used with this text are given in a separate place in chant books and carry no designation by occasion.

Although the Ordinary chants were originally congregational, the introduction of trained singers began, as we have said, a process of musical elaboration that led to both increased formal and musical complexity. In the Kyrie, for example, the text is a triple statement of the words "Kyrie eleison" ("Lord, have mercy") followed by another triple statement of "Christe eleison" ("Christ, have mercy") and concluded by another triple statement of "Kyrie eleison." At its simplest, this could easily be reflected musically by two melodies, repeated in the fashion AAA BBB AAA; curiously, only one Kyrie does this, that of Mass V. All the rest show the musician's talent for elaboration, for they range in formal complication from an AAA BBB CCC form (Mass VII) to ABA

CDC EFE (Mass III). Much the same situation can be observed in the Agnus Dei, in which one finds a simple triple repetition, AAA (Mass V), as well as a slightly more intricate ABA (Mass II) or ABC (Mass XI).

Performance of the Ordinaries is not strict as to antiphonal or responsorial manners, for either procedure may be followed. Alternation is the guiding principle, either between cantors and choir or between halves of the choir. In the Kyrie, for example, there may be alternation section by section, with the closing Kyrie ended by all, or alternation may exist within a section. In later centuries, with the introduction of polyphony, alternation was often made between sections in polyphony and in plainchant; this is seen in the Kyrie of the Mass by Guillaume de Machaut from the fourteenth century. There also developed a practice of alternation between choir and organ, but this did not become prevalent until the Renaissance.

The same process of alternation is followed in the Gloria, Credo, and Agnus; the Sanctus is performed by the whole choir, with an interruption at the Benedictus for the Elevation. The beginnings of the Gloria, Credo, Ite, and Benedicamus Domino are unusual in that, unlike any of the other chants, they are intoned by the officiating priest, not by cantors or choir. In these chants, the importance of the sacrifiant is so great that his place cannot be usurped by the musician. In the Gloria, the priest intones the opening, "Gloria in excelsis Deo," the choir entering only at "Et in terra pax hominibus." Similarly, in the Credo the priest intones the words "Credo in unum Deum"; the choir then proceeds with "Patrem omnipotentem." Only in later centuries, from after the 1700's, did it become common for composers to set these opening phrases. In performance of polyphonic settings from the Middle Ages and Renaissance of the Mass, these prefaces should be added by choosing chants from an appropriate mode to fit that of the work involved.

## ROMAN LITURGY—THE HOURS

The Hours, or Offices as they are sometimes called (not Office Hours!), are divided into two groups, the Greater—Matins, Lauds, Vespers, and Compline—and the Lesser—Prime, Terce, Sext, and None. All eight begin musically with the Psalm verse "Deus in adjutorium" ("Make haste, O God"), from Psalm 69, responded to by the second half of the verse and a Doxology. At the end comes a short "alleluia," except in Paschal Time, when "Laus tibi" ("Praise to Thee") is substituted.

Like all the Hours, Matins is primarily built around the singing of Psalms. After the opening, there is an Invitatory, with an antiphon acting as a refrain in the reciting of Psalm 94; this is then followed by a hymn, chosen in accord with the feast or season. The main part of Matins is made up of three Nocturns, each including three Psalms with framing antiphon and three read lessons. Each lesson is responded to by a Responsory, generally of considerable length and including as one of its verses the Doxology; in form the Responsory is much like the Gradual, except that part of the opening respond is inserted between the verse and the Doxology. In all, there are normally nine Psalms and nine Lessons; there may be, on special occasions, a "Te Deum" ("We praise Thee") at the end, either as an addition to or replacement for the final lesson. Of particular musical importance are the Responsories, for in the Middle Ages and after they were the inspiration for polyphonic settings. Also of interest is the fact that the Invitatory is an example of early antiphonal performance, in which the opening antiphon is repeated after each Psalm verse, not in the later framing manner.

Lauds and Vespers are basically similar in plan, being built around the singing of five Psalms, each with its own framing antiphon. A short lesson (Chapter) is read, followed by a hymn. There follow a verse and short response, leading into the singing of a Canticle, treated like a Psalm and with framing antiphon. The Canticle for Lauds is "Benedictus Dominus Deus" ("Blessed be the Lord God"), the Canticle of Zachary, while that for Vespers is the "Magnificat" ("May the Lord magnify my soul"), the Canticle of the Blessed Virgin. Vespers closes at this point, but Lauds adds as an ending one of the four Marian Anthems (or Antiphons) appropriate to the season; these four are "Alma Redemptoris Mater" ("Sweet Mother of the Redeemer"), "Ave Regina caelorum" ("Hail, Queen of Heaven"), "Regina caeli" ("Queen of Heaven"), and "Salve, Regina" ("Hail, O Queen"). These anthems are medieval additions, the result of the rise of the Marian cult; like the Canticles, they received later polyphonic settings.

Compline, the simplest of the Greater Hours, includes but three Psalms and one antiphon that frames all three. They are followed by a hymn, a Chapter with short Responsory and a Canticle, the "Nunc Dimittis" ("Now let Thy servant") or Canticle of Simeon, performed with antiphon as in Lauds and Vespers. The service closes musically with the appropriate Marian Anthem.

The Lesser Hours all have the same structure, a simple one suggesting their late introduction. Beginning with a hymn, they continue with three Psalms, all three using the same antiphon as a frame. There is also a Chapter with Short Responsory, together with a closing verse and respond. If Mass does not follow at Terce, the seasonal Marian Anthem is added to that service.

## ROMAN LITURGY—OTHER SERVICES

Standing outside the regular daily services, those determined either by their relation to Christmas or Easter, are certain special Masses, Votive and occasional, together with the Mass for the Dead. Votive Masses are generally intercessive in character and are usually celebrated only on those days when no other major feast takes precedence; their shape is the same as that given earlier. The same is true for certain occasional Masses, i.e., the Nuptial Mass and the Mass to Beg for Peace.

Of greater interest is the Requiem or Mass for the Dead, which takes its name from the opening words of its Introit, "Requiem aeternam dona eis" ("Give them eternal rest"). Its form is that of the normal Mass, the Gloria and Credo being omitted; its other Ordinary chants, however, are peculiar to it and are used nowhere else. Its most individual feature is the Absolution which may follow, containing a highly elaborate Responsory, "Libera me" ("Free me"), as well as the Canticle of Zachary with framing antiphon. The Requiem seems to have been the last major service to resist the unifying efforts of Rome, for the version as we find it today was generally accepted by the Church only with the Council of Trent.

## LITURGICAL SOURCES

The material of the Mass and the Hours is found in four volumes that are basic for the performance of services. The texts of the various Ordinaries and Propers of the Mass are given in the Missal, while the music for this service is printed in the Graduale. The components of the Hours are similarly divided, the texts appearing in the Breviary, normally split into four volumes by the seasons of the year, the music given in the Antiphonale. These last do not include the material of Matins, which is still in process of revision. For the benefit of smaller churches, a one-volume compendium was prepared during the late nineteenth century, the *Liber Usualis* (LU), which includes those parts from all four books that might have been performed in such churches, plus Matins for the great feasts.

Special collections of chants have been made, such as the *Vesperale*, containing material for Vespers and Compline, and the *Kyriale*, including Mass Ordinaries. One may also encounter volumes of chants later suppressed by the Council of Trent, the *Sequentiary* and *Tropary*, as well as others grouping chants by their musical mode, not by function, such as the *Tonarius*.

With the fundamental changes made by Vatican II in 1962 and the changes in the liturgy brought about by Pope John XXIII in the use of the vernacular in worship, the services as developed through the ages have drastically changed in shape and it is no longer possible to see in them all the long past and tradition that was once an integral part of the Catholic Church and its rites.

## MUSICAL CHARACTERISTICS

The systematic arrangement of a series of whole steps and half steps with reference to a tonal center is known in plainchant as a mode, in much the same way as later patterns are known as major and minor modes. Modes can perhaps be best understood by reference to a piano keyboard—one, however, without any black keys except B♭, with a range from G to e″, and with an untempered system of tuning based on but four basic proportions from which all else is derived, the kind of tuning known as Pythagorean (that described by Boethius). This tuning is derived from the use of four fundamental proportions, 2:1 (the perfect octave), 3:2 (the perfect fifth), 4:3 (the perfect fourth), and 9:8 (the major second). All other intermediate tones are derived from these basic elements by addition and subtraction; for example, the major third is in the ratio 81:64. Addition of proportions is done by multiplying the two numerators and the two denominators; substraction is done by multiplying the numerator of one by the denominator of the other. Thus, 9:8 added to 9:8 is gotten by $9 \times 9$: $8 \times 8$, or 81:64. The derivation of all these tones is described by most theorists with reference to the use of a single-stringed instrument called the monochord, on which the various proportional string lengths were laid out; Guido of Arezzo (990?–1050?) was the writer whose prescriptions were best known and followed. It was also Guido who defined in his *Micrologus* the number of notes and the total range used in music that we have mentioned above.

Taking then this keyboard and presuming its altered tuning, if we begin on d, play the white keys consecutively to d′ and then return to the starting d, we will have sounded the Dorian or First Mode. This mode we call authentic, with its range (*ambitus*) extending from final (*finalis*) to final; one note below the lower final may sometimes appear. If we begin on A, rise to a and return to d, we have the Hypodorian or Second Mode, whose range is from a fourth below the final to a fifth above; such

a mode, with its final in the middle of the range, is termed ░plagal░ As
with the authentic mode, one tone below the "lowest" may be used. The
other six modes are constructed in exactly the same way, beginning one
step higher for each succeeding pair; Example 2-1 shows all eight, together with their names and numbers; the *finales* have been marked with
an asterisk, with the added note given as a stemless black note.

**EXAMPLE 2-1.**

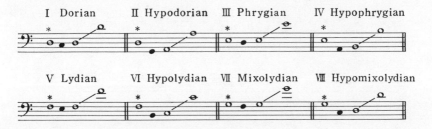

The names of the modes, implying Greek origins, in actuality have
no relation to the modes established by Greek theorists. Christian writers
adopted these terms under a series of misapprehensions; the Church itself
refers to each mode by number, not by name.

One may well ask here why it might not be possible to build further modes upon succeeding tones, that is, on a, b, and c'. This possibility
was broached by later theorists, principally by Glarean in his *Dodeca-
chordon* of 1552, using the names Aeolian and Hypoaeolian for Modes IX
and X (on a) and Ionian and Hypoionian for Modes XI and XII (on c').
Modern theorists describe a pair of modes on b (the Locrian and Hypolo-
crian), something never mentioned in the Middle Ages or Renaissance;
they were not then considered as a valid pair because of the inevitable
emphasis on the diminished fifth-augmented fourth, b-f, and vice versa.
Actually, the Aeolian and Ionian pairs are superfluous, since the substitution of a B♭ for B♮ in the First and Second Modes gives the same pattern
of whole steps and half steps found in the Aeolian-Hypoaeolian, and in
the Fifth and Sixth that of the Ionian-Hypoionian. Even when the B♭ is
used in a way to suggest the general shape of either the Aeolian or Ionian
pair, the designation in chant books is that of the appropriate one of the
basic eight modes; a good example is "In sole posuit" ("He placed in the
sun"), the Gradual for Saturday in Ember Week (Example 2-2). Here
(*LU*, 344–345), the mode is given as Hypodorian, although the final is a
and the range e-f'; evidently the mode is not Hypoaeolian, but a trans-
posed Hypodorian.

EXAMPLE 2-2.

In so - le po - - - - su - it * ta-ber-na - - cu - -
lum        su - - um:
et ip - se        tam-quam spon - sus
pro - ce - dexs de tha - - la - mo su - - o.

B♭ is used not only to allow for the transposition of modes, but also to avoid melodic difficulties caused by the tritone. The most obvious employment is that found in lines leading up from an F to a B and back; here B♭ normally replaces the B♮. No hard and fast rules can be laid down, however, for exceptions are both numerous and inconsistent. Much space was given to the problem by medieval theorists, all attempting to set up some sort of system that would help. Perhaps the best rule is that given by an anonymous theorist of the twelfth century: "Where a melody sounds most harsh, B♭ is stealthily inserted instead of B♮ to temper the tritone, but, where the melody returns to its normal nature, it should be removed." Any generality beyond this is sure to meet with contradictions.

Guido of Arezzo, of whom we have spoken in connection with the definitions of range and tuning, was also responsible for devising a system of sight-singing whose influence is still felt today. Guido noticed that the major problem for singers lay in understanding just where the half-tone interval was to fall in the various modes. To help remember the various scale steps, Guido utilized as a mnemonic aid a Hymn to St. John the Baptist, "Ut queant laxis," found in the Second Vespers for the Nativity of St. John (June 24), given here as Example 2-3.

In this hymn, each of the second through sixth phrases begins one tone higher than does the previous one, i.e., the six phrases begin in order with the tones C D E F G A. It was Guido's inspiration to recognize that, although the half-step, the crucial interval in the system, here occurred between the E and F, it also came at other points, between A and B♭ and

**EXAMPLE 2-3.**

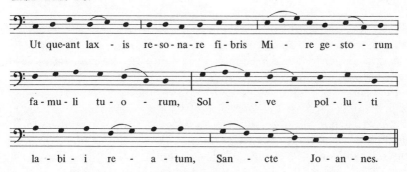

Ut que-ant lax - is re-so-na-re fi-bris Mi - re ge-sto - rum

fa-mu-li tu-o - rum, Sol - - ve pol-lu - ti

la - bi - i re - a - tum, San - cte Jo - an - nes.

between B and C. It was Guido's idea that one could use the St. John hymn as a way of universalizing these three situations by using the syllables that came at the beginning of each phrase as a way of remembering these crucial intervals: instead of using letters, one would use syllables, the ut, re, mi, fa, sol, and la of the successive phrases. Thus, the singer learned to apply these syllables to the music he sang, knowing always that there was a half-step between the syllables mi and fa wherever they occurred.

This set of six solmization syllables (for this is the name eventually given them) served the singer as a set of given reference points. The starting ut could be made on three different pitches, on C, G, or F. If begun on C, the half-step, mi-fa, came on E to F; if begun on G, the half-step logically appeared between B and C; if on F, the B♭ was inserted to give the half-step between A and B♭. If a particular melody extended beyond the limit of six notes (the hexachord), a series of rules prescribed how, depending on certain conditions, to shift from one type of hexachord and its solmization syllables to another; this shift was called mutation. To assist the student in remembering the mutations and the various syllables a note could receive, there grew up the idea of relating all these to the knuckles of the hand, where each knuckle stood for a particular pitch and for its various syllables. For example, C could be either the start of a hexachord on ut, or it could be the fourth note of a hexachord starting on G and thus called fa. This particular pitch would be then fully described as C fa ut, showing its place in both hexachords. The Guidonian hand as a help to memory was a part of nearly all elementary theoretical treatises to the sixteenth century; its basic elements, the syllables derived from the St. John hymn, are still with us in the study of sight-singing. In France, even today the use of letters as representative of pitches is not the custom; the derivations from Guido are the most common.

The hexachord system remained constant into the sixteenth century, although, with the rise of chromaticism and the increasing use of leading tones in polyphony, its utility was not as great. Although the system was extended to a full octave with the introduction of a seventh syllable in the fifteenth and sixteenth century (the ti or si), the hexachord's utility in the performance of plainchant has remained unchallenged. Even today, the singer who is thoroughly conversant with the solmization of the hexachord, its various starting points, and the rules for mutation will find that it is probably the only method to use in the correct performance of plainchant. To suggest the longevity of Guido's approach, one need but mention that possibly the clearest exposé of the fundamentals comes in the fifteenth-century treatise *Concerning the Nature and Propriety of Tones,* by Johannes Tinctoris, and that a whole school of notation in England, called the "tonic sol-fa" system, still publishes music written in sol-mization syllables, not in notes on a staff.

Plainchant melodies and formulae have many shapes, from the simplest intonations to the most elaborate musical expressions, all carefully tied to the function of enhancing the services in accord with the particular needs of the corresponding liturgical act. The most uncomplicated of these settings are those used in the intoning of the Prayers and Lessons of the Mass, known as the Common Tones. These are essentially recitations upon a single reciting tone, with slight rises and falls in accord with the normal variations of pitch made in reading the same text; these variations go no further than a third below or a second above the reciting tone and usually occur near the end of phrases. There is little musical individuality in these intonations, for the clear recitation of text is all-important; musical complication is not desired.

The formulae used for the chanting of the Psalms, the *psalm tones,* are somewhat more complicated, for, although their essence is that of recitation, they are not intoned by the celebrant, but by the choir, after an opening verse sung by a soloist to establish the pitch. This opening intonation is often a rise to the reciting tone or "tenor," with short changing-tone patterns at the end of each half verse (mediant) and full verse (termination) to emphasize the breaks in thought; succeeding verses do not repeat the opening phrase but begin immediately on the tenor. The tenors or reciting tones follow a general rule: in authentic modes, the tenor is the fifth above the final; in plagal, the third; where this would cause the tenor to fall on b, it is shifted a half step higher to c'. The tenor of Mode IV (Hypophrygian) is the only exception; its tenor is a. Thus we have the following:

| Mode | Tenor | Mode | Tenor |
|---|---|---|---|
| I Dorian | a | V Lydian | c' |
| II Hypodorian | f | VI Hypolydian | a |
| III Phrygian | c' | VII Mixolydian | d' |
| IV Hypophrygian | a | VIII Hypomixolydian | c' |

We see all these elements in Example 2-4, the opening of Psalm 112, "Laudate pueri" ("Praise, O Youth"), as sung to the formula for Mode II:

EXAMPLE 2-4.

We have noted earlier that psalms are performed with framing antiphons, more or less elaborate according to the service or feast. Since these antiphons appear in many modes, the choice of the psalm tone depends on the mode of the antiphon; if the antiphon required is in Mode I, for example, the psalm used will be chanted in the formulae of that mode. In addition, there must be a smooth transition from the closing of the psalm and the Gloria Patri used as the last verses to the beginning of the antiphon, now repeated as a coda. To make this possible many terminations are given in certain modes, designed to lead gracefully back into the antiphon; Mode I, for example, has ten of these.

The same approach may be seen in the formulae for the psalm verse and Gloria Patri used in the Introit. Melodies for each of the eight modes are provided, the mode of the opening antiphon determining that of the framed material. One should note that this is a set of special psalm tones, not the same as those used in intonation within the Hours; these are, by their place in the Mass, required to be somewhat more elaborate, although, as in the psalm tones of the Hours, the major emphasis is upon the tenor. In addition, there are alternative endings to the Gloria Patri, to make a smooth return to the beginning of the antiphon. The appropriate ending or difference (*differentia*) is specified by the music over the vowels EUOUAE, from "*seculorum. Amen,*" the closing words of the Gloria Patri.

The other chants of the liturgy, which can be considered as composed, generally derive their nature from the importance of the particular liturgical act that they accompany, the nature of the service, the importance of the particular feast, and the character of the text. Chants accompanying certain parts of the Mass, such as Communion, cannot be too long, for the celebrant cannot be kept waiting until the music is finished. Chants for the Hours tend to be less elaborate than those for the Mass of the same day; those for the Lesser Hours are normally simpler than those for the Greater. The celebration of a major feast, such as Christmas, usu-

ally contains chants of greater complexity and length than those for a
saint. Finally, differences are made in the setting of lengthy texts, such as
the Credo, and shorter ones, such as the Kyrie; too elaborate music for a
long text would take too much time. The composer did not work without
consideration of the balance of all these elements.

As an instance of the beauty found in the realization of even the
simplest of demands and as evidence of the composer's ability to achieve
an artistic result within functional necessity, let us examine the antiphon
"Scitote" ("Know thou"), from Terce for the Feast of the Holy Name of
Jesus (Example 2-5).

**EXAMPLE 2-5.**

8   Sci-to - te  qui-a Do-mi-nus ip-se est  De-us,  cu - jus   no-men in ae - ter-num.

This antiphon is evidently in Mode III, for its opening phrase, the
material to the asterisk, reproduces the opening of the psalm tone in that
mode; this much is normally all of the antiphon sung at the beginning.
Here, the direct imitation of what is to follow in the intonation makes the
transition smooth, for the rise to the reciting tone sets what is to follow.
Within the complete antiphon as performed at the close, there is an obvious intent to secure a graceful descent from this tenor to the final.
There is a steady fall in the second part, culminating in the repetitions of
the opening g at "Deus," a half cadence so to speak; after, there is a short
rise, then a steady descent to the closing e. Of great effect is the emphasis in the first part on syllabic treatment, with the use of a two-note
figure on "est" to stress the resting point; the conclusive nature of the latter part is assisted by the insertion of several of these two-note units at the
beginning of the section, with another just before the final helping to establish a sense of completeness. The effort to make the antiphon a significant introduction and satisfying close to the psalm recitation is evident
throughout.

As indicative of the distinctions made on the basis of function,
comparison between two settings of the same text is revealing. A particularly good example is the pair of chants on "Exiit sermo" ("The message
has been delivered"), the first the Respond of the Gradual, the second the
opening of the Communion for St. John (December 27) (Example 2-6).

In view of the function of the Gradual as the singing of a psalm,
accompanying no other act of the service, the composer felt himself comparatively free. As a result, the chant is highly melismatic, with many
notes to some syllables, and with evident effort to build a melody that will

EXAMPLE 2-6.

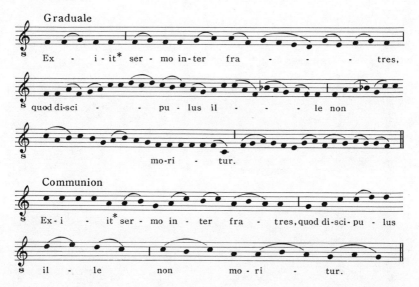

reflect the almost purely musical status of the Gradual. The Communion, accompanying a task of the celebrant, is by necessity of more restricted character, with a minimum of *melismata* and an almost purely syllabic treatment. In both chants we find a line that rises to a peak at about the middle, but the duration of rise to and fall from this climax is conditioned by liturgical circumstances, not by the wishes of the composer. Comparison of the two settings of "non moritur" points up the divergent demands, for, in the Gradual, this lengthy closing is governed by the evident desire of the composer to emphasize the meaning of "he will not die" by giving the phrase added musical importance. In the Communion, the need to coordinate the chant with the actions of the celebrant leads to a condensation which, while effective, is of lesser musical interest.

Of all the chants, the Alleluia is that most apt for the fullest musical expression. To medieval writers, it was an overpowering expression of the ecstasy of the spirit, a joy that could not be restricted to words; it thus occupied a peculiar place in the liturgy, for it carried implications of catharsis, a cleansing of the soul. This catharsis was not the result of the text but was derived from the music and its effects. Although a psalm verse is included, it too reflects the same approach, often repeating melodic fragments already heard in the Alleluia proper. As an example, we give the Alleluia "Vere tu es Rex" ("Indeed, Thou art the King"), for the Feast of the Holy Family (Example 2-7).

**EXAMPLE 2-7.**

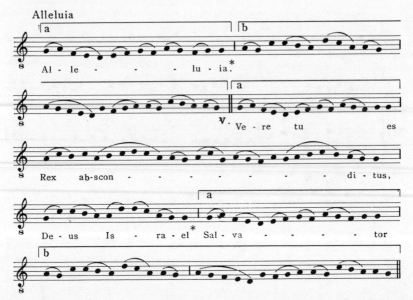

In performance, the opening to the asterisk is sung by a soloist, this then being repeated by the choir and continued to the verse; the latter part, from the asterisk on, is called the *jubilus,* and was to be of importance in the development of the type of chant called the sequence, as we shall see. The verse is then sung by the soloist to the asterisk, where the choir enters and completes it. There is then a return to the opening Alleluia, again soloistic, with the choir reentering at the jubilus; the choir does not repeat the opening Alleluia.

The Alleluia here is divided into three phrases, each ending on the final (Mode VIII), but each time more extended in length and in range, expanding almost like an opening flower. The first phrase is a preparation, firmly setting the modality, with the second and third phrases exploring the melodic possibilities. A major organizing factor is the use of a falling three-note figure that serves almost as a generator of melodic movement. The verse, in two broad sections, is closely related to the Alleluia, repeating the opening and closing phrases, marked *a* and *b* in the example. The intermediate section of the verse, the new material, similarly works with the falling three-note motive, giving a total unification to the chant that is both subtle and effective. Just as the second phrase of the Alleluia makes its ending inevitable, so does the new material of the verse make the repeated music of the Alleluia satisfying. Musical form and content are here in complete balance.

The artistry of the musicians of the early church rested on their solutions to the problem of balance between the claims of music and liturgy. Their ability to understand the demands of the function in which music played such a large part and to produce music that achieved its goal without sacrifice of musical value gave the West a secure foundation on which to base more elaborate musical structures. By their very success in merging liturgical function and musical accompaniment, we cannot think of the one without the other. Here the whole is greater than the sum of its parts.

## NOTATION

In the earlier days of the Church there was little need to worry about the problems of notation, for neither the complexity of the service nor its music was so great as to require that the various melodies or formulae be preserved in written form; comparatively few in number, they could be easily passed on through an oral tradition. With the Church's emergence and the rapid development of a highly organized liturgy, the problem grew more and more pressing, particularly when combined with the Roman rite's zeal to impress its procedures on all parts of the West. In taking chants from one area to another, some form of written notation became an absolute necessity. Although primary sources are lacking, it seems that the sixth century saw the first attempts to add some kinds of symbols to liturgical texts, indicating in a general way the course of the accompanying chant.

Many experiments took place in the ensuing three centuries, ranging from the use of specific letters or letter-like symbols for each note to the use of accent-signs taken over from those used in the teaching of oratory. There were, however, serious disadvantages in nearly all these systems, either because of an inability to know exactly the intervals specified or because of basic conflicts with the character of the chant; if one thinks of the essential nature of chant as melismatic, with groupings of notes more important than individual ones, it is obvious that a letter notation concentrating on separate tones would be more of a hindrance than a help.

The final solution, one achieved in its broad outlines by the ninth century and universally adopted in the centuries that followed, is based on the uses of two lines as reference points, the first, originally in red, to show the place of f, the second, in yellow or green, to indicate c'. The addition of other lines between and above or below, with the introduction of a clef, led directly to our modern five-line staff system; chant notation,

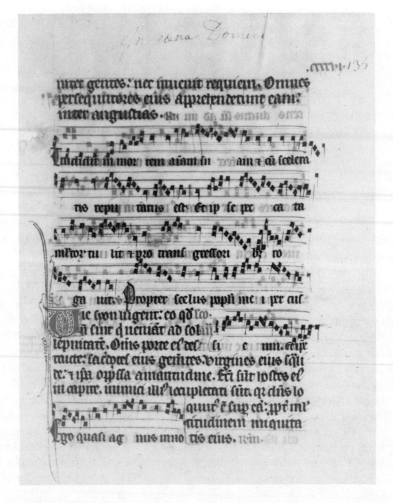

From the author's library. This music is for the Responsories to the second and third Lessons for Matins on Maundy Thursday. The liturgy represented here is non-Roman, from the north of France.

however, because of the restricted range of its melodies, had no need for more than four lines in its staff. While many older sources attribute the development of this to Guido of Arezzo, more modern research has shown that his role was more that of a codifier and improver of a system already in a high stage of development. Example 2-8 gives a short excerpt in neumatic notation, with transcription into modern form, to illustrate the method.

**EXAMPLE 2-8.**

In the example, the symbols at *a* and *b* are clef signs, the first indicating c′, the second f. At *c* and *d* we have examples of groupings, in which one figure stands for two or more notes. In reading obliques, one takes the first note from the point of its beginning, the second from its end. In cases such as at *d*, the bottom note is always read first. Comparison of the original and the transcription will make the principles clear.

The reader will have noted that nothing has been said about rhythm, and all our examples have implied that the notes are of equal value. In this lies one of the thorniest problems of plainchant, since we do not at present know specifically whether or not early chant had rhythmic variations and, if so, what kind. There is evidence that rhythmic distinctions may have been made in early chant books, but most of our sources come from after the ninth century, a period when these distinctions had begun to disappear from notated chants. The principal school of thought today, one accepted as standard by the Church, is that of scholars at the Benedictine abbey of Solesmes, in France, where the notes are of equal time value but with groups of two and three taken as units of pulse. Historically, the Solesmes procedure cannot be justified but it does lead to musically valid results. Other scholars have put forth schemes in which the notes are of varying length, but here again many of their results are open to debate. The problem is, at present, incapable of final solution, for there are too many unresolved contradictions in the sources.

## NON-ROMAN RITES

We have noted earlier that the early liturgical situation in the West was one of great diversity and that only after many centuries was the Roman rite universal. There were many causes for this situation, among them distance from Rome in a physical sense, the influence of local tradition and custom, the impact of foreign importations, and the changes brought about by the persistence of an oral tradition that often unwittingly resulted in major alterations. Regularization and conformation to purely Roman practice required the introduction of uniform liturgical

handbooks and notation as a method of preservation of authentic melodies, together with constant supervision by emissaries sent out by Rome
to oversee and purify local variations.

Even in Rome itself there existed a primarily oral tradition of
chant known as Old-Roman, seen today in manuscripts coming from the
eleventh century and representative of a tradition that seems to have
given way to Gregorian chant only in the thirteenth century. In Old-
Roman chant is found a kind of melismatic abundance not seen in Gregorian chant, perhaps suggesting a parallel development rather than one
rising to a peak and then cut off by the need for conformity to Roman
practice. The same type of melodic luxuriance can be found in what is
known as Ambrosian chant, a product of Milan, the city of St. Ambrose
(333–397), the legendary founder of its liturgical format. Efforts to sup-
press this Milanese rite were never successful and it is still in use today in
that city. The elaborateness of Ambrosian chant was thought to represent
an earlier stage in the history of chant, before Popes Leo the Great and
Gregory the Great; modern research indicates that the opposite is
probably true.

The earliest major divergence to disappear was that called the Gallican rite, that of France, for both Pepin and Charlemagne made strong
efforts to subject the French church to the dictates of Rome. Nevertheless,
certain of its elements, such as the "Improperia" for Good Friday, were
taken over eventually by the Roman liturgy. Today, all trace of the original Gallican chants is gone, for we have no sources from that time.

The Mozarabic rite, that of Spain, generally disappeared around
the eleventh century, although it is in use today by special permission in
certain churches of Toledo. The music, however, is not a true reflection of
the original, for, although many of the older sources have been preserved,
their notation cannot be read accurately. As one might expect, there is no
complete uniformity in the tradition and there were many variations from
one church to another, even though all did generally fall within the same
category.

Other minor chant variants have existed from time to time, showing many influences; certain ones reflect the impact of Byzantine practice,
coming from the Eastern Church. This kind of influence is particularly
strong in areas on the eastern coast of Italy, at places such as Ravenna,
where the East maintained its cultural dominance for many centuries. For
the history of later music, the most important local rite is surely that of
Sarum, stemming from Salisbury in England and in use throughout Britain by the fifteenth century. Its particular musical importance rests on its
use of certain chants later employed by Continental composers, as in the

"Caput" masses of Dufay, Okeghem, and Obrecht, plus its liturgy for the Requiem, one followed by most Northern composers of polyphonic settings until the Council of Trent. It was the last liturgical variation to fall before the supremacy of Rome.

## BIBLIOGRAPHICAL NOTES

In addition to certain sources already named at the end of Chapter 1, there are the many chant books published by Desclée & Co., Tournai, the authorized editors of the revisions made by the Benedictines of Solesmes; these include the *Liber Usualis* (1934), the *Graduale Romanum* (1938), and the *Antiphonale Romanum* (1924). Of special importance are the "Rules for Interpretation" given in the *LU*, pp. xvii–xxix, where the fundamentals of the Solesmes performance system are exposed. For studies of Gregorian chant, the many works of Peter Wagner are outstanding, as are the commentaries added to the various volumes of the series of facsimiles edited by the monks of Solesmes, the *Paléographie musicale* (1889–    ). Apel's *Gregorian Chant* has already been mentioned; his "The Central Problem of Gregorian Chant" in the *Journal of the American Musicological Society*, IX (1956), must not be overlooked.

For the history of plainchant notation, Carl Parrish's *The Notation of Medieval Music* (New York: Norton, 1957) is useful; the most extensive study is that of Dom Gregori Sunyol, *Introducció a la Paleografia Musical Gregoriana* (Montserrat: Abadia de Montserrat, 1925). Higini Anglés is also an important authority for this subject as well as for the history of non-Roman rites; his two articles in the *New Oxford History of Music*, II, should be consulted.

The best introduction to the Old-Roman rite is Paul F. Cutter, "The Old-Roman Chant Tradition: Oral or Written?", *Journal of the American Musicological Society*, XX (1967). An *Antiphonale Missarum juxta Ritum Sanctae Ecclesiae Mediolanensis* (Ambrosian rite) is published by Desclée (1935). The major present-day authority on Mozarabic chant is Don M. Randel; see his *The Responsorial Psalm Tones for the Mozarabic Office* (Princeton University Press, 1969); he has recently published *An Index to the Mozarabic Rite* (Princeton University Press, 1973). The question of Byzantine impact is taken up by Kenneth Levy, "The Italian Neophytes' Chants," *Journal of the American Musicological Society*, XXIII (1970). For the Sarum rite, W. H. Frere is the major authority; his various works, including facsimiles of both a *Graduale* (1894) and an *Antiphonale* (1901–1925), are essential.

# THREE

# ACCRETIONS
# TO THE LITURGY

In examining the liturgical make-up of the Mass and the Hours, one's first impression (a correct one) is that both have drawn primarily on Biblical sources for their texts. The emphasis on psalm-singing, the intonation of lessons from both the Old and New Testaments, and the stress on the Bible as a source for most of the material used within these services are clear. Those portions not Biblical in origin—the Ordinary of the Mass, for example—were not originally of the same importance or interest; we have already noted the subsidiary place of the Credo, which was not obligatory in the Roman rite until after the twelfth century.

This strong reliance on the Bible was not unconscious, for the Church early realized the necessity to discourage a subjectiveness inherent in the introduction of non-Biblical material. Although texts not drawing on the Bible were used in the earliest days of Christianity, mostly in the Eucharist, the growing Church rapidly suppressed them, acknowledging them as sources of possible deviation and heresy. The more solid the organization of the Church became, the greater was the official opposition to the introduction of non-Biblical writings.

Under pressure, such opposition could not and did not stand. For various reasons, to be explored in this chapter, non-Biblical accretions were slowly added to the basic liturgy, accretions more or less rapidly accepted and even at times encouraged by the Church. As a new outlet for the talents of poets and musicians, their vogue was great in the Middle Ages, so great that by the sixteenth century the Council of Trent felt that the essential focus of the liturgy had been obscured; many of the elaborations had to be trimmed away if the meaning of the services was to remain clear. During medieval times, however, these additions—the hymn, the trope and sequence, the liturgical drama, the conductus—attracted the attention of gifted men of poetry and music, for it was in them that these men could find a freedom of expression not always possible within the functional limitations of that which had already been established.

## THE HYMN

Of all the various liturgical accretions, the hymn is the oldest, for, as we have pointed out, it was part of the original Eucharist, non-Biblical in background, and partook of that same ecstatic emotion that was the source of the Alleluia. Because of its subjectiveness and individualism, it easily led into heresy, encouraging divisions and sectarianism, as can be seen particularly in the hymns written by the Eastern Gnostics, with Bardaisan (second century) as the leading spirit of the movement. These hymns, texts using popular melodies and folk tunes, were designed to teach religious doctrine and were polemic in nature. As a weapon against established dogma, their influence was great, calling for immediate reaction by the orthodox, one which grew rapidly after the third century.

With St. Ephraem (d. 379), the Church found its first great hymn writer. Like Bardaisan, St. Ephraem wrote in Syriac and, again like Bardaisan, used the hymn as a means of advancing certain viewpoints, but in support of the Church and not in opposition. Ephraem's major work is the *Madhrasa*, made up of poems against heretics, Bardaisan, and the Arians; songs of non-polemic nature on Christian moralities; and hymns of some liturgic connection. Many of these were incorporated into the monastic services that later grew into the Hours, thus defining a certain position for these compositions. As before, Ephraem relied for his music on popular melodies, insuring that the message of his texts would easily be absorbed by the singer.

Seeing the dangers in the spread of heresy through these easily sung and easily remembered compositions, the Western Church did its best to bar hymns from its rites; the Council of Laodicea, for example, around 361 banned them completely. However, such efforts were of little effect, for the popular character of the melodies to which heretical texts had been set and the insidious nature of the heresies themselves could not be fought by suppressing them.

The realization that the Latin hymn could defend orthodoxy in the same way as its Syriac counterpart was made first by St. Hilary of Poitiers (310?–366), who spent some time in exile in Syria and who may possibly have had personal contact with Ephraem. On his return to Gaul, he introduced the hymn there as a polemic weapon, fighting the Arianism then strong in Arles. None of his works, however, achieved great popularity, perhaps because of Hilary's failure to touch the masses.

The true father of the Catholic hymn is St. Ambrose (340?–397), for it is his work that established the model for future generations. Like Hilary, Ambrose's major goal was the combating of heresy. His success was complete—sung congregationally, his hymns immediately became popular and soon were absorbed into the liturgy, not only of Milan, Ambrose's bishopric, but also of other areas. Eighteen hymns now are believed to be his, but only four, named by St. Augustine, can be so definitely ascribed. Whether Ambrose also composed the music is not known; it is possible that, like his predecessors, he wrote his poems for already existing popular melodies.

An outstanding feature of the Ambrosian hymn is its emphasis on rhythm, indicating the shift from the older quantitative accentuation of classic Latin to the qualitative stress patterns of medieval Latin. The new poetry, truly Christian in both subject matter and technique, is rhythmic and eventually, in the hands of later artists, received rimes at the ends of lines. Divided into eight strophes, each strophe like two long lines of iambic feet, there is at the end of every two strophes a pause in textual sense, strongly suggesting antiphonal performance by the two halves of the congregation.

These elements then are basic to the hymn: 1) written to be a musical weapon against heresy; 2) popular in both words and music; 3) musically simple, with a strophic technique, that is, each strophe sung to the same music; 4) having congregational performance as a primary goal. To show these factors, we give the words and music of the first strophe of the Ambrosian hymn, "Aeterne rerum Conditor" ("Eternal Founder of all things") (Example 3-1), one of those named by Augustine as definitely by Ambrose; the melody is transcribed in triple rhythm, in accord with the qualitative nature of the poetry and specifications presented by Augustine in his *De Musica* (386–388):

EXAMPLE 3-1.

In general, to the eighth century, the Ambrosian hymn was the model. During this period, the steady absorption of the hymn into the Hours was constant, except in Rome, where there was resistance until the ninth century. In areas where certain poets were influential, such as France, or where the ecclesiastic character of the writer gave sanction, as in Northern Italy with Ambrose, the liturgical adoption of the hymn was rapid. Perhaps the most interesting feature of this change in position of the hymn is the change seen in the music, which began to take on the musical characteristics of normal plainchant; thereby it lost most of its rhythmic correspondence of words and music, for the new melodies to which hymn texts were set are stylistically closer to the highly melismatic chants of the already established service. They no longer have the clear rhythms of the past, and, without prior knowledge, it is difficult to identify a hymn melody as such. This may well be due to the monastic movement and its desire to make the Hours more solemn by the addition of hymns, something requiring a higher degree of musical sophistication than the original folklike melodies; this goal is particularly evident with the Irish Benedictines.

A good sample of the rapidity with which the character of the hymn changed can be seen in "A solis ortus cardine" ("From the rising point of the sun") (Example 3-2), sung at Lauds on the Feast of the Nativity of Our Lord. Its text was written around 450 by Sedulius, an Italian or Spaniard probably working in Achaia. Only eight strophes are used by the Roman Church (*LU*, 400–402), although the original poem, in praise of Christ, contains twenty-three; each strophe begins with a succeeding letter of the alphabet, that is, the first has as its first word "A," the second "Beatus," the third "Clausae," and so on through the alphabet, omitting J, U, and W, these not being part of Latin orthography. The whole text, to be found in Stephen Gaselee, *The Oxford Book of Medieval Latin Verse* (Oxford: Oxford University Press, 1946), is used in the Mozarabic rite.

EXAMPLE 3-2.

A so - lis or - tus car - di - ne   Ad us - que ter - rae

li - mi - tem, Chri - stum   ca - na - mus Prin - ci - pem,

Na - tum Ma - ri - a   Vir - gi - ne.

With some slight jamming together of the melismata, the hymn could possibly be sung in triple meter, for the poem has the same metrical shape as "Aeterne rerum Conditor," with the use of rhyme in the scheme *abba*. But it is obvious that the characteristics of plainchant have begun to make such a procedure unlikely. In places there are just too many notes to allow compression into a strict metrical scheme (as at the end of the third line). The composer of the music is here more intent on a broad melodic sweep, working from a beginning that almost echoes the idea of the sun rising to a high point in the third line, "We sing of Christ the Prince," and falling to a rest in the final line. The use of five notes to one syllable is unusual for the hymn, for most have no more than two or three.

The hymn remained a constant source of inspiration throughout the Middle Ages. With the expansion of the choir school in France under Charlemagne, the new centers, such as Paris, Tours, Dijon, Fleury, Chartres, and Auxerre, not only assisted in the unification of the area under the Roman rite but provided the atmosphere for the continued creation of the hymn. Their work made of the hymn not only a way of fulfilling a now obvious liturgical function; it also gave it the status of a recognized art form, of interest to future generations.

A typical example of the later hymn is "Pange lingua" ("Spread, o tongue, the mystery of that glorious body") (Example 3-3), for Second Vespers of Corpus Christi (*LU*, 957–958), whose text is by the great Catholic theologian, St. Thomas Aquinas (1225–1274). The opening line is an imitation of an earlier hymn by Venantius Fortunatus (530–610), for the Mass of the Presanctified on Good Friday (*LU*, 709–710). St. Thomas was much concerned with the service for Corpus Christi, furnishing for it also the hymn "Verbum supernum prodiens" ("Coming as the heavenly Word"), based on another earlier anonymous hymn from between the fifth

**EXAMPLE 3-3.**

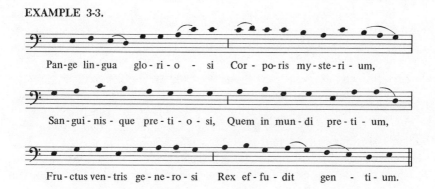

Pan-ge lin-gua  glo-ri-o - si  Cor - po-ris my-ste-ri - um,

San-gui-nis - que  pre-ti-o-si,  Quem in mun-di  pre-ti - um,

Fru-ctus ven-tris ge-ne-ro-si  Rex ef-fu-dit  gen - ti- um.

and eighth centuries, as well as a sequence to be noted later and the sermon for the day.

As with "A solis ortus," the composer has endeavored to give a clear melodic shape to his creation, here with a rapid rise to a high point at the beginning of the second line, emphasizing the word "Corporis" as essential to the meaning of the day. From this climax there is a steady but gradual fall to the end, with the scalewise descent in the last line bringing the piece to a satisfying close. Not only is this one of the Church's great hymns, but its importance as a source of inspiration for later musicians should also be noted: it serves as the foundation for one of Josquin des Prez's most often-performed works, the "Missa Pange lingua," first printed in 1539. Another chant melody is sometimes used for the hymn (*LU*, 950–952); the one given here is that used by Josquin.

## THE SEQUENCE AND TROPE

Just as the hymn acted as a creative outlet within the Hours, so the sequence and trope acted within the Mass. Although the total number of sequences now found in the liturgy has fallen to five and the trope has completely vanished, both were very important forms in medieval times, losing their preeminent position as musical categories only with the rise of polyphony as an area of greater interest.

The background of the sequence is hidden in obscurity, although it now is evident that the original inspiration was of Byzantine provenance. In the East, it had long been the habit to adapt new texts to previously existing melodies, much as the earlier Syriac hymn writers had used popular songs for their new texts. With the presence of many Greeks in France during the ninth century, it is probable that knowledge of this custom became expanded in that part of the West. Regardless of exactly how and when the idea was transmitted, it is certain that shortly after 862 a monk from Jumièges in Normandy appeared at the monastery of St. Gall in Switzerland, driven there at a time of troubles in his homeland. Among the baggage of this monk was a small volume of chants in which additional texts had been fitted to the long melismata that make up the *jubilus* of the Alleluia, the melismata on the final *-ia*, which were then longer than those now found in today's chant books. One of the St. Gall monks, Notker (840?–912), recognized that the added text might well serve to aid the singer in remembering the involved *jubilus* melodies. With the advice and encouragement of his teacher, Iso, Notker attempted to provide what he considered more suitable texts, working from the principle that the original melismata should be broken down into individual notes and each note thus derived provided with a syllable.

From this story, related by Notker in the preface to his *Liber Hymnorum*, it is evident that the procedure of adding words to an already existing melody was not a new one and that the original exploration of its possibilities was primarily a result of French experimentation. This practice, known as *prosula* technique, may be found in manuscript sources from the ninth century on. One of these, Paris, Bibliothèque Nationale, lat. 1118, from the tenth or eleventh century, shows how extensive this practice was, for it contains 91 prosulae, for parts of both the Ordinary and the Proper. Some utilize in the proses for the Alleluia all of the music, not only the opening Alleluia but also the verse or combinations thereof. There was no set procedure except that the writer used musical material already present, with nothing new provided.

Notker may well have found that this procedure was not sufficiently artistic, for it is not followed so strictly in his own productions. Although many of his sequences can be specifically tied to the melismatic Alleluia, many cannot, suggesting that at this early stage in the history of the sequence its ties to the Alleluia were somewhat tenuous and that, in Notker's view, the sequence had not become set in its liturgical position. Unlike the French, the St. Gall writers wrote poetry of rhythmic character, not prose, and neglected the use of lines ending in *-ia*, derived from the final syllable of Alleluia. This technique of not only providing new words to an old melody in places, but of composing new music to go with new words as a kind of insertion, is called *troping*, with the sequence in its mature form acting as a trope for a particular part of the Mass, the Alleluia. Notker already shows the unwillingness of the musician to be confined so closely as required by the procedure of the prosula.

The original sequence, as we have seen in the prosula, was closely tied to the melismatic *jubilus* or the verse of the Alleluia. It was originally a poetic creation, not a musical one. With the extension given by troping, the form began and ended with isolated strophes, with pairs of strophes in between, thus producing a structure known as the *double cursus:* X–AA–BB–CC . . . Y. The melodies for the opening and closing isolated strophes, as well as for each inner pair, were different; the number of syllables from one pair of strophes to the next was not constant, giving great irregularity to individual line lengths.

The technique of the prosula provided so little room for the imagination of the artist that it is no surprise that the sequence did not long remain attached to the Alleluia melodies, although it did retain its liturgical position at that point in the service. Melodies now began to be freely composed, with no relation to the *jubilus*, although retaining the syllabic character and musical form of the original. By the late tenth century, the musical reliance on the Alleluia had been completely broken, as in the Easter sequence, "Victimae paschali laudes" ("Praises to the Paschal victim"), of Wipo of Burgundy (d. 1050); the present-day version (*LU*, 780) has slightly obscured the form by omission of the original sixth strophe.

One further development, arising out of a French love for symmetry and balance, may be noted: the gradual elimination of differences in length of strophes. The great figure in this change is Adam of St. Victor (d. 1192), a member of that Augustinian monastery founded by William of Champeux (1070–1121), the teacher of Abelard. With Adam, all strophes have the same regularity and formal balance, thus eliminating the external signs of the double cursus. Now, only reference to the music can make clear the difference between the hymn and the sequence, for the poetry is superficially the same; the hymn, however, is strophic in its music, while the sequence retains its double cursus idea, with new musical material for each pair of verses.

At the peak of its popularity, the sequence became an almost universally adopted part of the Mass, even appearing in those seasons in which, because of its joyful character, the Alleluia was substituted by the Tract. Large collections of sequences were put together in special volumes, laid out like the Graduale. Sequences thus became organized much like the Proper of the Mass, with specific ones for specific days. Just as in the history of the Proper, there was a definite effort on the part of successive generations to fill out the church calendar, to differentiate between various feasts by the degree of intricacy of the sequence, and to accentuate the minor differences in ritual between one church and another. Inevitably, this led to an individualism, a subjectiveness, that later caused the Council of Trent to remove all but four sequences from the liturgy: "Victimae paschali laudes" (*LU*, 780), for Easter Sunday; "Veni sancte spiritus" (*LU*, 880–881), for Whitsunday; "Lauda Sion" (*LU*, 945–949), for Corpus Christi; and "Dies irae" (*LU*, 1810–1813), for the Requiem

Mass. The first, "Victimae," has already been mentioned as by Wipo of Burgundy in the eleventh century. "Veni sancte spiritus," sometimes known as the "Golden Sequence," is probably by Cardinal Stephen Langton, Archbishop of Canterbury (d. 1228). "Lauda Sion" is by St. Thomas Aquinas, and "Dies irae" is usually credited to Thomas of Celano (d. 1250?), the friend and biographer of St. Francis of Assisi. A fifth sequence (*LU*, 1634–1637), the "Stabat Mater" of Jacopone da Todi (d. 1304), was reintroduced in the eighteenth century as part of the Feast of the Seven Dolours of the B. V. M.

The trope, like the sequence, began as a prosula, with the addition of words to a preexisting melody in such parts of the Mass as the Introit, Kyrie, Gloria, Gradual, etc. The Paris manuscript mentioned above contains, for example, prosulae for 22 Offertories. The trope seems to have had much the same origins as the sequence and, like the latter, was first really exploited at St. Gall through Tuotilo, a friend and contemporary of Notker. Thus we have two types, the one using a given melody and providing a new text or texts for it (the prosula), the other taking the standard chant and its accompanying text, breaking it into sections and interposing new bits of melody and text in the spaces made available. A manuscript at Sens (Bibliothèque Publique, 46) shows the extent to which this latter practice could be used: the Mass for the Circumcision of Our Lord found in this source begins with a Kyrie or a traditional chant, but to it is added a prosula beginning "Clemens rector, aeterne pater." In the Gloria, Credo, Sanctus, and Agnus Dei, there is a true troping process, in which both melodic and literary insertions have been made. In the Gradual, a long insertion, like a commentary, is placed between the first two words of the original text, and, in the Benedicamus, a series of short strophes has been placed at the beginning, before the original text is announced.

In essence, the technique of troping—the idea of adding to an already existing foundation—is common to both sequence and trope, but there is one major difference: the trope is bound in meaning to the text to which it is added, while the sequence has no such close connection. The use of the trope as explanation was carried quite far; we have twelfth-century examples of certain Epistles in which there is an alternation of the original material in Latin with its text in French translation, for the benefit of the less learned.

By the thirteenth century, the vogue of the trope was nearly at an end, and three centuries later all tropes were banned by the Council of Trent. It might be noted, however, that modern chantbooks do head certain Kyries with the opening of the trope that was once used with them; for example, the Kyrie of Mass IV is named "Cunctipoters Genitor Deus" ("God, the All-Powerful Creator").

Within the trope one finds the typically medieval procedure of glossing. The *gloss,* an explanation or exegesis, is the use of a basic authority on which a new structure is built by the addition of commentary. In many manuscripts, the original text is written with large spaces between the lines; between these lines, the commentator could (and did) insert his explanations and definitions of the original text, seeking to clarify every possible meaning and implication. The old serves as the inspiration for the new, acting as a source of authority to which the new makes constant reference. The trope is the musical equivalent of the gloss in literature and logic.

## THE LITURGICAL DRAMA

If one looks today in the *Liber Usualis* for the text of the Passion according to Saint Matthew (*LU*, 596–599), one will notice that the text is interlarded with extraneous symbols, a cross and the two letters, C and S. This is an indication to the reader that he is to give this text in more than one tone of voice: the words of Jesus, those prefaced by the cross, are to be read in a low voice; those of St. Matthew (prefaced by the letter C) in a medium voice; and those of the others, the crowd of the Jews and the Disciples (S) in a high voice. (The letter C stands for the Chronista, the Evangelist; the letter S stands for the Synagoga or, as it is sometimes called, the Turba or crowd.)

To assign these three roles to three different performers was not a great step and, in the Middle Ages, it became the tradition to perform the Passion in this manner. Although lacking action or staging, this manner of chanting the Passion story was the ancestor of the liturgical drama.

For a second source of the liturgical drama, one must look again to St. Gall, where, among the works attributed to Tuotilo is "Hodie cantandus" ("Today we must sing"), a trope-like introduction to the Introit for Christmas. This composition began with one choir singing "Today we must sing of the Child," followed by the second choir asking "Who is this Child? Tell us. . . ." To this, the first choir replied "He is that Child . . . whom the prophet has foretold," with the Introit immediately following the last phrase. As before, there is within this germ the medieval desire to explain and amplify, for, as St. Ethelwold says in his *Regularis Concordia*, written between 965–975, this enlargement of the service is ". . . to fortify the faith of the ignorant multitude and novices. . . ."

Beginning as a musical dialogue, the range of the drama soon broadened to include action and scenic representation, although the essential character of the question-and-answer formula was not discarded. In the "Quem quaeritis" for Easter, these elements were combined into a complete play. On Good Friday, the Cross, wrapped in veils, was deposited on an altar representing the Sepulchre. Before Matins on Easter Day, sacristans removed the Cross, leaving only the veils; during Matins, one monk carrying a palm branch took his place in the Sepulchre. After the third Responsory, three other monks approached the Sepulchre, carrying boxes of incense; on being asked by the monk there, "Whom do you seek?" they replied, "Jesus of Nazareth." The first monk then stated, "He is not there; He has arisen," to which the three responded by turning to the choir with the words, "Alleluia, the Lord is arisen." To the phrase, "Come and see the place. . . ." the three inspected the Sepulchre, leaving their incense boxes and showing the veils to the choir. After the singing of "The Lord is arisen from the Sepulchre," the "Te Deum" was begun, with ringing of all the church bells.

The above description is found in the *Regularis Concordia*, and it represents what was happening all over Europe, for the custom of introducing drama within the liturgy, particularly at Christmas and Easter, took rapid root. The original short versions were rapidly expanded, with additional scenes and dialogue to heighten interest and make the message more vivid. At Easter, for example, the extensions might include the preparation of the three Marys for their visit to the tomb, the purchase of incense or the visit of Simon and Peter; the resources of the church involved would determine the degree of complexity and splendor.

With the expansion of the drama came a similar enlargement of possible subject matter, although there was not the universality of the schemes for the Nativity and Easter. These new subjects, generally found from the eleventh century on, include episodes from the lives of saints, such as St. Nicholas, and passages from both Old and New Testaments, such as the "Play of Daniel," "The Conversion of St. Paul," "The Raising of Lazarus," and "The Last Judgment." The popular character of the liturgical drama is suggested by the use of the vernacular in certain ones, such as in the "Play of the Wise and Foolish Virgins," from Limoges in the mid-twelfth century; the text is part Latin and part the dialect of Limousin. Finally, there is a "Play of St. Agnes" from the fourteenth century, written in Provençal; strictly speaking, this does not fall within the category of liturgical drama, for it is a play with incidental music based upon popular melodies or variations on the hymn "Veni Creator" ("Come, O Creator").

In the sources, the music for the various liturgical dramas is written as plainchant, but it is not impossible that improvised counterpoint was added at climactic points; such a procedure would have been in keeping with the grandiose presentations that are suggested. It is also probable that instruments of various kinds played a strong role in these performances, to judge from various descriptions that have come down to us. The music itself is generally syllabic, with short melismata often coming near the end of the phrase. To a certain extent, there is a correspondence in style between the melodies of the liturgical drama and those of the hymn of the same time. While the poetry used is normally metrically organized, the accompanying chant often ignores this rhythm, for a stressed syllable may receive but one note, an unstressed melisma many. Evidently these melodies were performed in the manner of plainchant; as an example we give the opening of the "Quem quaeritis" as it appears in Padua (Biblioteca Capitolare) C 56, of the fourteenth century (Example 3-4):

EXAMPLE 3-4.

Quem quae - ri - tis in se-pul - chro    Chri - sti - co-lae?

Certain other melodies suggest a more popular character, using a syllabic setting that strongly implies rhythmic performance. In these, there are few melismata and the general appearance is that of the Ambrosian hymn, although the iambus has been replaced by the trochee. Such songs were probably performed metrically in triple rhythm. In the "Play of Daniel," from twelfth-century Beauvais, there is something of an effort to distinguish between music for soloists, to be performed like plainchant, and material for the choir, which is rhythmically organized and of less melismatic character.

The popularity of liturgical dramas in the Middle Ages was great, but little artistic development occurred after the fourteenth century, although they continued to be performed into the sixteenth century. With the transfer of dramatic composition to the secular world, dependence on music as an integral factor virtually disappeared; what little music was used in church dramas came to be secular in origin and was more in the nature of interpolated songs rather than part of a musically conceived whole. One may suggest that the difference between the liturgical drama of the high Middle Ages and its secular derivatives was something like that between opera at the Metropolitan Opera House and musical comedy on Broadway.

## THE CONDUCTUS

A final liturgical accretion, brought about by functional needs, was the conductus, its name implying music to accompany a procession; the term seems to have been first used in the "Play of Daniel," where it was applied to the pieces sung at entries. In addition, the term was applied to the music introducing the closing "Benedicamus Domino" of Vespers and Lauds. The place of conductus in the Church can be compared with that of the trope; just as the trope was an elaboration of a particular chant, the conductus was an elaboration of a liturgical act, a heightening of it by music.

Like those of the hymn, the strophes of conductus are uniform, but here the musical resemblance ends. Formal structures are much more varied, although there may be the strophic procedures of the hymn; other methods include through-composition, with constantly new music, the double cursus of the sequence, and even forms borrowed from the secular, such as the rondellus and ballade.

Conductus as it appears in the services has generally the musical characteristics already seen in the late hymn; the poetic rhythm of the text is often ignored by the composer, for long melismata sometimes fall on unstressed syllables. Conductus seem to have been composed with a definite effort to make them fit stylistically with the plainchant of the rest of the service.

Of all the liturgical accretions, the conductus was freest in its creation, for it did not take its beginning from a musical demand of the liturgy. It was, therefore, a category with few restrictions on either text or music. As such an expression, its artistic relations reached outside the Church; one assumes that the musical and poetical characteristics of the conductus had existed long before its liturgical use as processional music. The name is a late addition, based on its function alone. As a monophonic artistic creation, it had a secular history, to be discussed in the next chapter; as a polyphonic type, it held an important place in the music of the thirteenth century, to which we shall turn later.

The interest in sacred monophonic composition reached its peak in the late twelfth century and declined rapidly thereafter. With the rise of polyphony and the growth thereby of increased artistic opportunity, the interest of musicians rapidly turned to the newer techniques, with the goal of re-ornamenting with polyphony all those areas that had been so carefully elaborated in plainchant over preceding centuries. We can look back in amazement at the complexity and variety of what is, to many modern ears, the barest of materials, the single musical line. Yet, within this simplicity we find the essence of medieval thinking, the elaboration of a world of complicated reasoning resting on a simple assumption.

# BIBLIOGRAPHICAL NOTES

As a source for the general background of all the poetic types mentioned, F. J. E. Raby's *Christian Latin Poetry* (Oxford: Oxford University Press, 2nd ed., 1953) is basic. It may be supplemented by F. Brittain, *The Medieval Latin and Romance Latin Lyric* (Cambridge: Cambridge University Press, 1951).

The music for the hymns is generally available in the various chantbooks already named, plus Bruno Stäblein's *Monumenta Monodica Medii Aevi*, I (*Hymnen*) (Kassel: Bärenreiter, 1956); Vol. III of this collection (1970), edited by Günther Weiss, is devoted to tropes for the Introit. When complete in ten volumes, the *Monumenta* will be a major source for the principal monophonic forms of the Middle Ages. For the sequence, two collections give an idea of the range of the music: H. M. Banister and Dom Anselm Hughes, *Anglo-French Sequelae* (London: Plainsong and Mediaeval Music Society, 1934), and Dom R.-J. Hesbert, *Le Prosaire de la Sainte-Chapelle* (Mâcon: Protat Frères, 1952), a facsimile of a thirteenth-century collection. The liturgical drama is best seen in those edited by Noah Greenberg and W. L. Smoldon and published by the Oxford University Press. Many examples of conductus are given by Friedrich Gennrich, *Lateinische Liedkontrafaktur* (Darmstadt: Gennrich, 1956), and in the facsimile edition of Florence, Biblioteca Medicea-Laurenziana, Pluteo 29.1 (Brooklyn: Institute of Mediaeval Music, n.d.), folios 415 to the end.

For the prosula, sequence, and trope, the major authorities are Jacques Handschin and Hans Spanke, both writing in German. A good survey of the sources, with excellent examples, is Ruth Steiner, "The Prosulae of the MS Paris, Bibliothèque Nationale, F. Lat. 1118," in *Journal of the American Musicological Society*, XXII (1969). Richard L. Crocker has done important work in this field and his many articles on the subject should be consulted; they appear in various journals, but one should note especially those in the *Journal of the American Musicological Society*, XI (1958) and XX (1967). Crocker is presently preparing a study of Notker and his contributions, which will include the music. For liturgical drama, E. K. Chambers, *The Medieval Stage* (Oxford: Oxford University Press, 2 vols., 1903), and Karl Young, *The Drama of the Medieval Church* (Oxford: Oxford University Press, 2 vols., 1933), are essential. The latest researches are due to W. L. Smoldon, with particular reference to his article in the *New Oxford History of Music*, II. For the conductus, Leonard Ellinwood's "The Conductus" in *Musical Quarterly*, XXVII (1941), is still of value.

# FOUR

# SECULAR MONOPHONY

The study of non-liturgical monophony to the twelfth and thirteenth centuries contains many problems and complications that cannot
allow final answers. That there must have been a great quantity of non-
religious music during these ages is a truism, for we have intimations of
its importance in the history of the hymn: the adaptation of popular
melodies to new poetry of sacred character implies the existence of a
large stock of music without relation to liturgical purposes. And we find
mention of music in connection with purely secular activities, so that we
can be sure that it played an important role in the everyday life of the
time. Nevertheless, our knowledge is both skimpy and uncertain.

A major reason for this is the almost complete lack of written
records. If music (and its allied poetry) were to exist for future generations, it needed to be copied into manuscripts and then preserved in
some kind of library. In view of the laborious processes and the length of
time required, and the expense of materials needed, a natural tendency

of those who directed the scribes was to emphasize that which was most essential in their eyes. Since the preparation of manuscripts was the exclusive province of the trained cleric, working either within a monastery or a royal court, the result was an almost complete neglect of all that did not contribute to the functioning of one or the other establishment. Within the monastery, emphasis fell on the copying of material for the liturgy, religious tracts of various kinds, and instructional works in all those areas needed for religious training. Within the courts, major effort was spent on correspondence and items directly tied to the process of government, with passing attention to chronologies, history, and laudatory poems. Viewed as lacking in seriousness and meaning, secular productions received scant attention and were not normally considered worthy of preservation.

A second factor is the background of what was preserved, for it reflects principally one social group, the clerical circles that had sufficient education to write down their achievements. If we remember that the skills of reading and writing were restricted to a comparative handful, and that this handful was part of the religious segment of society, then it can be understood that those works we do have are, in the main, representative of that class and no other. Only when social conditions had begun to change and the nonclerical person had begun to have something of the same education as the cleric could there be any preservation of great numbers of compositions from men not of monastic background.

Finally, there is the question of musical notation, often a secondary matter in the minds of the scribes and therefore omitted. Even when included, because of the slow development of accurate methods many of our earlier sources are not in precise notation; in all too many cases, we can only be sure that there was music to accompany certain texts; from the indefinite character of the notation used it is impossible to define the melody. In certain cases, there is even the implication that the melody to be sung was so familiar that it did not need to be indicated, a familiarity that does not exist for us today.

With all these factors at work, the secular music preserved from these early centuries is certainly not a complete representation, for it is far too fragmentary and inadequate. The poetry is in Latin, the language of but one class; the music is indefinite, although implied. In most cases, we can only infer and suggest; we cannot be certain.

## LATIN SECULAR MUSIC

In the beginning, sacred and secular monophony are exceedingly difficult to separate. Those men whom we know to have been the major representatives of secular creation, men such as Venantius Fortunatus (530?–609), are part of both worlds, reflecting both the religious and the laic; their poetic and musical forms indicate that they were highly influenced by those developed within the liturgy. While much of the poetico-musical activity took place in Southern France, in Provence and Aquitaine, important centers also existed in Northern Italy, in Bobbio and Verona. The two latter monasteries, founded by the Irish monk, St. Columban, were extremely productive in the seventh through ninth centuries. Perhaps their most important achievement was the development of refrain forms, to be taken over later by works in the vernacular.

With the period of Charlemagne, the ninth century, a certain rebirth of interest in the Latin classic made its appearance. From this time come musical settings of such works as Boethius's *Consolation of Philosophy,* certain of the Horatian *Odes* and parts of Virgil's *Aeneid;* because of the notation used, they are indecipherable. With this looking backward, there also came an enlargement of subjects treated, to include love songs, songs of praise, and laments. There is within all these an implied necessity for music even when music does not appear with the text. Also included within these texts are descriptions of instruments of the time, suggesting the growth of instrumental accompaniment to vocal pieces.

The most important secular Latin products of a slightly later time are the compositions produced by the Goliards or wandering scholars. These men, clerics who roamed from one university to another as they pleased, show in their works the naturalism of the young, their subjects ranging from the most chaste of love lyrics to the most obscene of drinking songs. Preserved principally in a Cambridge manuscript of the twelfth century and a thirteenth century manuscript from Benedictbeuern known as the *Carmina Burana,* these poems show the mixture of sacred and secular forms and rhythms to be expected from those whose training has been religious but whose lives were spent outside religious establishments. While musical notation appears in both sources, it is of an early type that will not allow transcription. Certain melodies can be supplied from later sources, where the notation is more advanced, but they are not sufficient in number to give a complete picture.

There is, however, a strong suggestion that many of the melodies used by the Goliards were of sacred origin, a not implausible source in view of the custom of troping. We have one secular piece, "O admirabile Veneris idolum" ("O lovely image of Venus"), which uses as its melody that of a processional hymn, "O Roma nobilis" ("O noble Rome"). It is probable that many others were arrived at by the same process, termed *contrafactum,* by which new texts were supplied as replacements for the old; this technique is well within the medieval tradition of building on the pre-existent.

## TROUBADOURS AND TROUVÈRES

Under the onslaught of successive waves of barbarians and the varieties of languages brought with them, Latin as a means of communication at all levels of society began to weaken. Although it remained the language of the Church and of educated men, it steadily assumed less and less importance for those outside clerical circles, for secular society turned to those variations brought about by the impact of the invaders. While this process was going on all over Europe, the first evidences of an effort to elevate the new languages to carriers of artistic intent were seen in France, where two strong movements can be discerned.

The first of these, found in Southern France from around the middle of the eleventh century, is that associated with the language now known as Provençal or the *langue d'oc;* its musician-poets are known as troubadours. The second, in Northern France and rising from the middle of the twelfth century, used the language variation at the root of modern French, the *langue d'oïl;* artists working in this tongue are called trouvères. In both cases, the names suggest connection with the older process of troping.

The major center for the growth of early troubadour art was around Poitiers, the seat of the Duke of Aquitaine; one may recall that from this area came also both Hilary and Venantius Fortunatus. As a part of that duchy and with a chateau for the Duke, Limoges in Limousin also acted as a secondary center, with much cross-influence between the ducal establishment and the monastery of St. Martial. In time, the troubadour influence spread through most of southern France, covering the basin of the Garonne to Toulouse and Narbonne. These areas were generally unified by their political outlook as well as their language; a certain kind of civilization arose there that was conducive to the production of art of all kinds.

This new civilization was one of leisure, without the necessity of continual combat to protect itself. Influenced by the Church and its desire to keep peace (except against the Church's own enemies), the knights of Provence found themselves attached to their castles in a life of comparative ease. With this new leisure for men came leisure for women and a change in the relations between the sexes, with an exaltation of the place of the lady in noble society. As a way of showing greatness, a lavish scale of living became the custom, with attention to display in clothing, furniture, housing, food, drink, and all other pursuits of enjoyment. Among these pastimes, the art of the troubadour soon took a high place, for, within this new framework, the achievements of a noble musician-poet could give him the same high reputation that preeminence in battle could have given in previous times.

The first important representative of the new spirit was William IX, Duke of Aquitaine (1071–1127), of whom eleven works are preserved, with a fragmentary melody for one. These pieces show the broad characteristics of those to follow, among them the understanding that these songs are intended for an aristocratic audience and that the poetry is to be expressive of the feelings of the author, subjective reactions to the topic involved. In later generations this subjectiveness led to a deliberate obscurity of expression, even to the use of coined words; the best representative of this tendency is Arnaut Daniel (1180?–1210?), much praised by Dante.

The principal subject of troubadour pieces is love in all its various aspects; indeed, the forty poems we have of Bernard de Ventadour (after 1150) are built on nothing else. In addition, there are dialogues in the manner of debates, wherein a subject is proposed and two viewpoints are exposed in alternation; this poetic contest, perhaps modeled on real ones, is the *tenso, partimen,* or *joc partit.* A third broad category is the *sirventes,* taking up almost any subject except that of love. Among its subtypes are the Crusade song, the political satire, and the *planh* on the death of a protector or friend. These songs were not normally performed by the creator but by a special class of musician known as the *jongleur.* The jongleur was not a composer or poet, but merely a performer who made his living by going from place to place and displaying his talent before any social level that would pay him. Although the great mass of jongleurs remained servants, members of the lower classes, some few were lucky enough to be received into the castles, where their talents were at the service of the nobility; these men were known as minstrels. They were expected to please their various audiences and therefore had large repertoires of almost every type of musical entertainment. Not only did they sing the short creations of their betters but they also gave much attention to the long epic poems of the time, the *chansons de geste* of which the "Song of Roland" is the best known example; these were sung to short melodic formulae that fitted the rhythmic patterns of the poem. In addition to accompanying themselves instrumentally, they were also expected to provide music for dancing, with acrobatics and juggling as supplementary diversions.

The art of the troubadour disappeared at the beginning of the thirteenth century, with the destruction of Provençal civilization in the Albigensian Crusades that began in 1209 and ended twenty years later. With the conquest of Southern France by men of the North and the consequent political and social upheavals, the class that had brought forth the troubadour vanished. By the end of the thirteenth century the last troubadour, Guiraut Requier (1235?–1292), had brought the story to an end; even he spent the last years of his life in Spain, under the protection of Alfonso X.

Contact between Northern and Southern France had been constant for many centuries, and many troubadours, Ventadour and others, are known to have visited Northern courts during the twelfth century. The Crusades too caused many meetings between the nobles of both areas, occasions on which the troubadour art was demonstrated. By the mid-twelfth century the exchange had become sufficiently effective that certain Northerners began to imitate in their own language the work of their Southern masters. These first productions were little more than changes of language, following Southern technique and content almost slavishly. Indeed, admiration for troubadour models was so great that many of the most highly esteemed were later quoted in trouvère works.

Most recent research has shown that neither the troubadours nor the trouvères emphasized a particular group of musical forms to accompany their poems. In the minds of both groups, the music occupied a secondary role and served as a vehicle for the text; on the whole, there is little formal unity between the two elements. Easy classification is impossible. Nevertheless, the thirteenth century did see the rise of what have been called the fixed forms, the *rondeau,* the *virelai,* and the *ballade;* in the case of the rondeau in particular, it is of some importance that the earliest ones we have do not come from the troubadour or trouvère repertoire, but seemingly from a lower social level, the bourgeois segment of society. It does seem probable that the ancestry of the virelai and ballade may be traceable to the troubadour and trouvère production, but the problem still is not completely solved, and as yet there is no sign of ultimate clarification; too much depends on what one takes as a definition of the form as a standard for this early period, that before the thirteenth century.

The thirteenth century, however, does see the regularization of these three forms, and they came to dominate both poetry and music for the next three centuries, until the opening years of the 1500's. In its classic form, the rondeau began with a refrain of a full strophe, followed by a half-strophe and a half-refrain; after a succeeding full strophe there was a return to the full refrain to close the work. Musically, there were but two fragments, one for each half-strophe and repeated in accord with the poetic text; the full diagram is ABAAABAB. The ballade was normally in three strophes of seven or eight lines each; the last one or two lines of each strophe are identical and act as a refrain. The musical form is AAB, each A standing for two lines and the closing B the remaining ones; this form is much like the *canzo* of the troubadours. The third form, the virelai, begins with a refrain of a full strophe, followed by two half-strophes (the *ouvert* and the *clos*), a full strophe (the *tierce*), and finally the full refrain. Musically, the form is ABBAA, with each A representing a full strophe, each B a half.

Preservation of poetry and music of both troubadours and trou-

vères has been comparatively plentiful, for we have approximately 2500
troubadour poems and 250 melodies, with over 4000 trouvère texts and
some 1400 melodies. In view of the high social distinction accorded to
gifted nobles, it was felt appropriate that collections (*chansonniers*) be
subsidized by them for presentation purposes or for simple glory. It may
be presumed that the copyists were clerics attached to the household.

The music for troubadour and trouvère songs is generally simple,
frequently syllabic and normally with short melismata, much like the hymn.
The influence of the modes is apparent, although there is a tendency to
introduce accidentals in such a way as to suggest more of our modern
major and minor. The range is usually limited, seldom going to the octave.

As to rhythm, there has been and continues to be constant debate.
One group, that most influential in the past half-century, has argued that,
in view of the rhythmic nature of poetry, the music too, regardless of its
notation and usual lack of clear rhythmic definition, is to be transcribed
in patterns, these derived from the metric structure of the poem. This
solution might be more convincing if the poems themselves were rhythmically regular from line to line, but they are not. As a result, it is almost
impossible to find two authorities making identical transcriptions of the
same work. As a sample of the melodic style and one possible rhythmic
interpretation, we give here a short troubadour work in honor of the
Virgin Mary (Example 4-1), taken from a twelfth-century manuscript
originating at St. Martial in Limoges; the reader must remember that the
notation of the original makes no distinction in shape from one note to
another and, in fact, is very much like plainchant:

EXAMPLE 4-1.

O Ma - ri - a   deu mai - re,   Deu   tes   e   fils   e
pai - re, Dom-na   pre-ia per nos,   To fil lo glo-ri - os.

The second group argues that the lack of rhythmic indication in the
note shapes means that these pieces were done in free style, that some
form of rhythmic notation would have been used if the songs had been
performed with rhythmic patterns; according to this argument, the scribes
employed the form of notation that most closely approximated the actual
manner in which the songs were heard, i.e., freely declaimed without
reference to a particular pattern. One might think of this practice as a

kind of recitative, not as a carefully organized melody. As a sample of this viewpoint, we give the same piece as it appears in the original source but transcribed in the manner of the plainchant examples given earlier (Example 4-2).

**EXAMPLE 4-2.**

O Ma-ri-a    deu mai - re, Deu tes e fils e pai - re,

Dom-na    pre - ia per nos,    To fil lo glo - ri - os.

## SECULAR MONOPHONY IN ITALY

With the Albigensian Crusade and the consequent confusion, many troubadours fled to other parts of Europe. One of the preferred refuges was Northern Italy, an area already visited by many Provençal artists during the late twelfth century; particularly important was the court of the Marquis of Montferrat, who had received Peire Vidal (1175?–1205?) and Raimbaut de Vaqueiras (1155?–1207?). Raimbaut's works show the international character of the troubadour, for he is the author of a *descort* with its first five strophes successively in Provençal, Italian, French, Gascon, and Galician-Portuguese; the sixth, of ten lines, repeats the order of languages in its five paired lines. Raimbaut is the writer of the earliest known poetry in Italian (1202).

The Italian *trovatori* of the North generally followed their troubadour masters closely, not only taking over their techniques but also their subject matter. A few Italian poems are almost literal translations of Provençal models, although the more usual derivation is that of a transfer of imagery. More originality is found in the output of the South, for under Frederick II (1211–1250) Sicily became a major center of development. The climax of the process of development of an individual Italian approach came only at the end of the thirteenth century in Central Italy, with Dante (1265–1321) as the real founder of Italian literature.

No music for any of these Italian courtly songs has survived, but a great number of hymns in the vernacular have remained. Known as *laude spirituali*, these were the result of a spiritual revival climaxed by the work of St. Francis of Assisi (1182–1226) and were designed for performance by

the lower classes. Written in a popular Italian, the *laude* show the influence of chant, but secular elements are also apparent. In form, an Italian
equivalent of the virelai—the *ballata* (not to be confused with the ballade)
—is normal, although the music may not be as simple as its French counterpart; there are often fresh melodies in each section.

A typical example of the category is "Fami cantar" ("Let me sing
the love of the Blessed Virgin"), a strophic song of which we give only the
first two lines (Example 4-3). The style is that of the hymn, essentially
scale-wise with only a few small skips.

**EXAMPLE 4-3.**

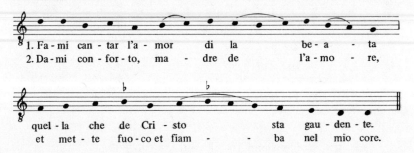

```
1. Fa - mi can - tar l'a - mor      di  la        be - a   -   ta
2. Da - mi con - for - to,  ma  -   dre de        l'a - mo  -  re,

quel - la   che  de  Cri - sto               sta  gau - den - te.
et   met - te  fuo - co et fiam  -     -     ba   nel  mio core.
```

## *SECULAR MONOPHONY IN SPAIN AND PORTUGAL*

The situation in Spain and Portugal was much like that of Italy,
for the various courts of the Iberian peninsula had long had close connections with those of Southern France. Peire Vidal was one of the close
friends of Alfonso II of Aragon, and other troubadours had become well
known in Castile and in Portugal. As in Italy, the earliest productions
were extremely close to their sources in all facets, with the rise of peculiarly Iberian manifestations occurring only in the thirteenth century; even
here, there were some reproaches for failure not to follow the Provençal
models closely enough.

Preservation of a Spanish-Portuguese repertoire of purely secular
music has been poor, for only six songs in Galician-Portuguese have survived with their music. What has come down to us is a collection of
Marian songs, the *Cantigas de Santa María,* settings of poems relating
miracles performed by Her. Although the *Cantigas* are all anonymous, it
is probable that certain ones are by Alfonso X (1221–1284) of Castile and
Leon, for the collection was put together at his court. Many of these songs
reflect French influence, the whole group recalling the *Miracles de Notre
Dame* by Gautier de Coinci (1177–1236). In form the majority follow the

outlines of the *villancico,* the Spanish equivalent of the virelai. Example 4-4, a song in praise of the Blessed Virgin Mary, shows the form and musical characteristics.

**EXAMPLE 4-4.**

## SECULAR MONOPHONY IN ENGLAND

In spite of a close connection between England and the continent, there seems to have been little response to troubadour influence. During the late twelfth century, parts of Southern France were possessions of the English crown through the marriage of Eleanor of Aquitaine to Henry II, and the presence of troubadours at the English court was common;

Bernard de Ventadour visited there. Indeed, Eleanor's son, Richard the Lion-Hearted, became a practicing trouvère; his death in 1199 was mourned by Gaucelm Faidit (1180?–1220) in a moving *planh,* the only one whose music has come down to us.

The failure of troubadour art to call forth extensive English reaction lies in the great gulf between the Norman nobility, speaking a variation of French, and the rest of the country. Not until England could develop an individual language of literary capability could there be great progress; this did not occur until Chaucer's time. Nevertheless, a few simple melodies with English texts have remained, generally syllabic and with scale-wise motion as a major characteristic; there is much repetition of similar fragments, suggesting an approach to melody through formulae.

## MINNESINGERS AND MEISTERSINGERS

As in the other parts of Europe, Germany felt the influence of the troubadours early, during the late twelfth century. Exchanges were facilitated principally by the Crusades and also by frequent visits of troubadours and trouvères to Northern Europe; these visits extended quite far, for Peire Vidal is found at the Hungarian court of Emeric around 1200. Intermarriage was also of importance in furthering cultural exchange, one outstanding example being the wedding of Beatrice of Burgundy to Frederic Barbarossa in 1156.

On the whole, as descendants from the troubadour-trouvère tradition, the Minnesingers remained close to their teachers. Recent research has indicated that the early development of Minnesinger poetry is almost completely imitative, with few individual touches; themes, techniques, forms, and imagery are all closely tied to French originals. Perhaps this explains the comparative poverty of musical sources, for it is probable that the first Minnesingers not only took over all the poetic characteristics of their teachers but their melodies as well; one Minnesinger tells us that his lady had sent him an untexted French melody to which he should supply a German text.

Whether or not there was originally a direct taking over of French melodies, it is certain that German forms followed closely those developed in the South. Of particular importance was the German equivalent of the ballade, the *Barform,* with its *Stollen-Stollen-Abgesang* form, so eloquently described by Hans Sachs in Richard Wagner's *Die Meistersinger* more than five centuries later. Other forms included imitations of the troubadour patterns, the *Spruch* following the *sirventes,* the *Geteiltezspil* the *joc partit,* and the *Leich* the *descort* or *lai.*

Later Minnesingers show a greater individuality, although a reliance upon French models is always in the background. The peak of the movement comes somewhat late in comparison to other areas, the closing thirteenth and early fourteenth centuries marking the high point. After this time the Minnesinger art declined rapidly, passing over into bourgeois society as imitation of upper-class customs. This movement within the middle class was undertaken by the group known as the Meistersingers, a guild-like organization that survived into the early nineteenth century. Although the Meistersingers were theoretically both poets and composers, the emphasis fell most strongly on the poetic side, for the major efforts were devoted to the provision of new poetry for a stock of traditional melodies. Musically, there was little viable in the Meistersinger movement, for it represented an effort to take over an activity of an upper social level by a middle class to whom it was artificial and at a time when it no longer held artistic possibilities.

It is significant that the full flowering of secular monophony came at a time when monophony was no longer of great concern to musicians within the Church. With the steady development of polyphony, the attention of professional church composers and performers turned to the new technique, for it made a greater appeal to their artistic talents. As a result, the provision of new monophonic works within the Church was left increasingly to the less trained, to the amateur not able to work with the new complications. The task of providing the liturgy with a new polyphonic adornment, replacing or supplementing older monophony, was sufficiently challenging and intriguing to cause a comparative neglect of further expansion of the sacred monophonic repertoire by the professional; he turned to polyphony.

The amateur status of monophony in the twelfth and thirteenth centuries is reflected by the taking over of this area by the secular musician-poet working in the vernacular, a man with little of the musical background common to the church-trained. A musical novice, he perforce fell back on what he had heard—chant and popular melodies—without going further. For him, the area of greatest interest was not the music but the poetry. The very notion of a stock of melodies, a group of formulae, to which many poems could be set implies this lowered place of music, as does the failure to preserve melodies and poems in equal quantity. Even in those cases in which the music is of some artistic significance, and there are many, there is still a sense of reliance upon an already developed artistic foundation, one carried to a peak by church musicians of the past.

Together with the failure of monophony to maintain its previously high artistic position goes its consequent drop in philosophical importance. In treatises of the time, the place of monophony becomes more and more a demonstration of certain fundamentals whose philosophical meaning is intensified when absorbed into polyphony. In a nutshell, polyphony demonstrated the meanings of speculative music better than did monophony and thus stood on a higher level. Whereas Guido had given considerable space to directions for composing simple monophony, thirteenth-century theorists used the same space on directions for improvising simple polyphony.

With the failure of sacred monophony to continue its expansion in the face of the rise of polyphony, it is no surprise to see the Church turning to secular productions when it needed monophony for particular purposes. Stylistically in accord with the already existing repertoire because of their background, secular monophonic works could be and were provided with new texts to fit a new function. Many thirteenth-century monophonic conductus were so derived, and numerous other works were given Latin religious *contrafacta,* for the continuation of monophonic composition in secular circumstances gave ample stocks of melodies to satisfy the Church's requirements. In time, many of these were made part of later polyphonic compositions, for the custom of providing *contrafacta* in both directions, from sacred to secular and vice versa, gradually destroyed any feeling on the composer's part that any melody necessarily carried connotations of the text to which it had been originally fitted. It became to him but a musical element, to be used in a musical construction and handled in the same fashion regardless of whether its origin was sacred or secular. All of this is but one facet of the increasing secularization of the Middle Ages, to which we will return later, in our discussion of the polyphony of the thirteenth century.

Like the decline of monophony in the Church, the disappearance of secular monophony may be tied to the rise of polyphony. Just as monophony fell to a second place in the Church, so did it drop in secular circles. With an appreciation and understanding of the superiority of polyphony, the secular composer endeavored to carry over the new technique into secular areas. Secular monophonic works within the upper social levels disappeared first in those areas such as France, where polyphony made its first gains; in Germany, where polyphony developed late, it remained long after it had vanished almost everywhere else.

Of course, secular monophony never completely vanished. Perhaps a better phrase would be that it lost its artistic significance for the social class that had originally fostered it. As of lower artistic import it remained a manner of musical expression at lower levels of society, either as imitation of their betters or as an artless expression in musical terms. The folk song survived, as it always had and always will, but it was no longer taken as worthy of professional attention and elevation. Art music henceforth was to be polyphony, something not capable of composition by anyone without thorough grounding in its techniques. In monophony, the amateur might compete, but in polyphony he could not.

## INSTRUMENTS AND INSTRUMENTAL MUSIC

As we have seen, the early Church Fathers were deeply opposed to the use of instruments within the liturgy, regarding them as too much a part of pagan culture. As such, they had no place within a Christian life and were to be shunned by every believer. Some exceptions were made from time to time, such as a certain acceptance of the lute and kithara because of their relation of King David, but these were always understood to be special cases. In spite of Biblical reference to the trumpet, cymbals, and other instruments, their relation to Greek and Roman society was such as to inspire mistrust.

With the split of East and West and the continual influx of barbarians ignorant of the music of the past, the matter of forbidding instruments became simpler; most of those under suspicion had disappeared and those in use had no connotational problems. In the course of time, there was a general tendency to forget many attitudes of the past and to accept the use of instruments as part of the musical scene. While many instruments were indigenous, coming from various parts of Europe and especially from the outer edges, some were importations from Asia via the many contacts that we have already noted. By the tenth century, instruments were an acknowledged part of musical practice and, to judge from our sources, had standard symbolic meanings.

So far as the Church was concerned, the most useful of all instruments was the organ. Although the Romans had developed a form of organ called the *hydraulis,* from its reliance on water pressure, the medieval organ or *positive* was supplied with air from a bellows, worked by either hand or feet. The choice of tones was not governed by a keyboard in the earlier examples but by a series of slides that opened and closed the appropriate pipes. A true keyboard as we know it was not developed until the twelfth century, but mechanical friction made the action so stiff that it required a full-fisted blow on the key to cause the sound. In spite of the primitive state of engineering, attempts were made to enlarge the organ's possibilities, one instrument of the tenth century at Winchester being built with 2 manuals, 26 sets of bellows, and 400 pipes. Early organs were loud and not in tune; nevertheless, the positive became an important part of the Church's music, so much so that all other instruments were eventually banned (for a time) from services. By the fourteenth century, the organ had assumed a place in the symbolism of the time as "the king of instruments," a term used even today and derived from both its sound and its place in worship.

A form of easily transported organ, the *portative,* became part of the music at court. Small and capable of being worked by one man without assistance, it carried none of the religious associations of its larger

Rome, Vatican, Rossiano 455, folio 1 recto. The text is the opening of the *Declaratio musicae disciplinae* by Ugolino of Orvieto. At the right, from top to bottom, are pictures of cherubs playing various instruments: the vielle, the lute, the portative, the psaltery, and the hurdy-gurdy. The illuminated initial shows an artisan building an organ. At the bottom are singers grouped around a music book.

brother. Since one hand of the executant was occupied in building up the air pressure, its function was not that of a polyphonic instrument but of a monophonic member of chamber combinations.

Together with the portative were associated many other monophonic instruments of varying types and methods of sound production; these include the harp, the psaltery, and the lute (plucked stringed instruments) and the vielle and the rebec (bowed instruments). Although the harp had a long history, the one used by the Middle Ages was brought from Ireland where it had the connotations of a royal instrument; it appears even today in the Irish coat-of-arms. By the late twelfth century it had lost something of its position, for it was then the instrument favored by jongleurs and wandering actors. Both psaltery and lute were originally brought to Europe by the Moors in Spain and slowly spread to the rest of the continent. Curiously, both were not normally plucked by the bare finger but by a quill or rod; the goal seems to have been a certain impersonality of tone.

The vielle, like the harp, was primarily an instrument used by the jongleur to accompany the *chanson de geste* or to provide music for dancing. Although usually played with the bow, it could be plucked. One of the more celebrated secular works of the twelfth century, "Kalenda Maya" by Raimbaut de Vaqueiras, was the result of the troping of an *estampida* played for him on the vielle. The rebec, an instrument of Arabian origin, is the distant ancestor of our violin, although its original shape suggests a relation to the lute; in the thirteenth century, it had but two strings, tuned to C and G.

Two groups of instruments, the brass and percussion, were the particular property of the nobility. Of highest significance was the oliphant, a horn most often made of an elephant's tusk, although sometimes found in gold; its Eastern origin is obvious. As a symbol of nobility, it was carried by a knight as part of his standard equipment; it could not belong to any other class. It was an oliphant that the dying Roland sounded at Roncesvalles, and certain medieval miniatures show it as being used by the Archangel Gabriel at the Day of Judgment. The trumpet, in wood or brass, also served as a military instrument, used on all grand occasions. Together with the timpani, brought to Europe in the Crusades period, it was symbolic of a royal presence and its players were given precedence over other instrumentalists of the court. Its functions in war were similar to those in later periods.

There is sufficient evidence to prove that instruments were a normal part of almost all musical performances, but the music itself gives no clue as to how instruments took part. Modern performances of medieval music have attempted to reconstruct as well as possible the original conditions, but there can be no final guarantee of authenticity. About all that we can be certain of is that medieval audiences liked varieties of instruments, not homogeneous choirs. In Guillaume de Machaut's description of a concert from the fourteenth century, 31 different instruments are listed as part of the orchestra, and a total of more than 50 players in the ensemble is implied. The music as we find it in the sources suggests none of this. Indeed, we have no firm ideas of how monophonic music was accompanied, although we are sure that it was; in all likelihood, the accompanying line essentially duplicated that of the singer, with occasional added ornamentation, in what is called heterophony.

The earliest independent instrumental pieces in our sources come from late thirteenth-century English manuscripts and are dances for one instrument. The most interesting of these is the *stantipes,* formally organized in the double cursus of the sequence. Derivations from this form can be found until the early Renaissance, in both French and Italian sources. That even the few examples we find have survived is surprising, for the place of the dance in the Middle Ages was such that copying of these works was not to be expected; in the manuscripts in which they appear, they are obvious afterthoughts.

Some polyphonic music for instruments has been preserved, the most important being two codices of keyboard music from the fourteenth century, the *Robertsbridge Codex* of English provenance and the Italian *Faenza Codex.* Both contain sacred and secular works in idiomatic arrangements and show an effort to add figurations and ornaments to give the work a more instrumental cast. Both sources make it evident that truly independent instrumental music was only at its beginnings and that vocal music was the center of creative activity.

## BIBLIOGRAPHICAL NOTES

Although he says little about the music, F. J. Raby's *History of Latin Secular Poetry in the Middle Ages,* 2 vols. (Oxford: Oxford University Press, 1934), is essential; nor should one overlook Helen Waddell's *The Wandering Scholars* (New York: Doubleday, 1955). Jack Westrup's "Medieval Song," in the *New Oxford History of Music,* II, is extremely helpful on all aspects of secular monophony and includes many examples.

For the poetic achievements of the troubadours, H. J. Chaytor, *The Troubadours* (Cambridge: Cambridge University Press, 1912), although dated, is still one of the best sources in English; Robert Briffault's *The Troubadours* (Bloomington: Indiana University Press, 1965) is also of importance for its excellent translations and provocative discussions of ancestry and later impact. So far as the music is concerned, the older tradition of scholarship is represented by the work of Jean Beck, Pierre Aubry, and Friedrich Gennrich; unfortunately, little of their work is available in English. Beck and Gennrich have both supervised the preparation of facsimiles of some of the sources. The new attitude toward transcriptions of this repertory is represented in Hendrik van der Werf, *The Chansons of the Troubadours and Trouvères* (Utrecht: A. Oosthoek, 1972). This is a major study and cannot be overlooked; it contains comparative transcriptions of fifteen troubadour and trouvère chansons, with excellent English translations of the texts.

For a good survey of trouvère achievements, see Jessie Crosland, *Medieval French Literature* (Oxford: Basil Blackwell, 1956). Both Beck and Aubry have published several volumes of trouvère compositions. Theodore Karp's article, "Borrowed Material in Trouvère Music," *Acta Musicologica*, XXIV (1962), is a fascinating study of cross-relationships; in addition, Robert H. Perrin's articles in the *Journal of the American Musicological Society*, IX (1956) and XVI (1963), should be noted. On the use of fixed forms in this music, see Willi Apel, "Rondeaux, Virelais, and Ballades in French 13th Century Song," *Journal of the American Musicological Society*, VII (1954).

Early Italian music is best presented by Fernando Liuzzi, whose *La Lauda e i primordi della melodia italiana* (Rome, 1935) is an outstanding achievement. Gennrich has prepared several small volumes of facsimiles of Minnesinger works for his classes at Darmstadt; these give a thorough idea of the style. A complete transcription of the *Cantigas* is available: Higini Anglés, *La Musica de las Cantigas de Santa Maria* (Barcelona, 1943).

For the history of musical instruments, Curt Sachs's *The History of Musical Instruments* (New York: Norton, 1940) is basic. Edmund A. Bowles has published several articles on the place of instruments in the Middle Ages; these appear in *Acta Musicologica*, XXXIII (1961), *Revue de Musicologie*, XLII (1958), and *Archiv für Musikwissenschaft*, XVIII (1961). A facsimile of the Faenza Codex is published in *Musica Disciplina*, XIII–XV (1956–1961); a complete transcription with extended commentary has been published by Dragan Plamenac, with the vocal originals that have been traced (Rome: American Institute of Musicology, 1973). On the problem of instruments in the Church, James W. McKinnon, "Musical Instruments in Medieval Psalm Commentaries and Psalters," *Journal of the American Musicological Society*, XXI (1968), is essential.

# FIVE

# THE BEGINNINGS OF POLYPHONY

If one had to define in a few words the characteristics that set the music of the West apart from that of other cultures, the first point to be made would be, in all probability, the simultaneous performance of many individual melodic lines, all generally under the control of the composer. While other civilizations do have music with a multitude of individual lines sounding at the same time, it usually relies upon improvisatory skills of the performers, not the guiding hand of the inventor. In these cultures, there is not the easy possibility of duplication of performance, the repetition of the same work in the same form and shape as in its original creation; in most of them, the starting point is not a completed composition, but a simple scheme to guide the performers in their individual elaborations, without pre-existing complications.

Although Western polyphonic music began from this point, its history has been marked (until very recently) by the steady growth of the composer to a commanding position over the performer. The development of notation, the introduction of tempo markings and dynamic signs, the explanation of interpretation by verbal directions, the technique of orchestration, all these things and others are direct indications of the ever-increasing domination of the creator over the reproducer. That many composers of today have turned to electronic means and the computer (without intervening interpreters) is but a logical conclusion to the historical process of the past, the steady growth of the composer's control over the interpretation and performance of his musical creations.

The beginnings of this process in the Middle Ages show little of what was to come, for early polyphony owed its start to the improvising performer. Where the inspiration for this new technique, eventually called counterpoint from its note-against-note characteristics (*punctus contra punctum*, to give the Latin), originated has not been satisfactorily settled. Many theories have been advanced, but no hypothesis has yet been given that has brought general agreement. Some scholars have suggested that the ancestry may lie in Greek music, where is found a technique of two performers improvising on the same melody, or heterophony. Others have supposed that its roots rest in the natural variations in voice placement from one person to another; they theorize that the same melody sung by tenor and bass at the same time, both using the most comfortable parts of their ranges, would produce a series of parallel intervals resembling the products of early polyphony. Further hypotheses include an origin in folk music, a result of chance discovery, or the outcome of philosophical speculation on the possibility of simultaneous interval performance. Perhaps the only certainty may be that polyphony in one form or another existed elsewhere before it grew in the West; it may well be that, like the hymn and so many other liturgical additions, polyphony was imported from the East.

Regardless of origin, by the seventh and eighth centuries a simple improvised counterpoint had developed to such a point that writers were beginning to mention it in terms that imply that it was a common practice. Our earliest remarks come from a treatise on Latin prosody from England, by Bishop Aldhelm (640?–709), who refers to *organum,* the term for this elementary note-against-note technique, as a symbol of well-arranged metric accent. He also notes that organum was of particular value for joyful occasions; this attitude toward polyphony, that it could serve as a musical discriminant within the liturgy by setting off an occasion of importance, was a major factor in its later development. There is also a ninth-century statement that Roman singers imported to France by Charlemagne in 787 taught the fundamentals of polyphonic improvisation to their students there. Most authorities do not take this report seriously, for it is probable that its author was trying to justify the use of polyphony by referring its derivation to the heart of the Church; the whole episode seems to be the product of imagination rather than fact. When, at last, technical descriptions of polyphony began to appear in theoretical works by the ninth and tenth centuries, we find in them no effort to trace its history or to attach it to particular regions; evidently, it was of sufficient age and universality to be considered a custom, not a novelty.

Like the other accretions to the liturgy mentioned earlier, the beginnings of counterpoint are found in the various monasteries of the West and their attached choir-schools. Indeed, the same religious centers important in the development of the sequence and trope were also those where polyphony rceived its first impetus, and the placing of an additional line of music against one already given is in the same tradition as literary troping, where an addition of a text is made to a pre-existing melody. Western polyphony, in its earliest stages, was no more than musical troping and, like its literary brother, another form of that reference to authority so much a part of the medieval mind. The given melody, the basic plainchant, was that authority to which commentary, now in musical terms, was added. As in the history of the literary trope, the musical trope or polyphony was to undergo an expansion that would go far beyond a complete reliance upon the given material; even though the added material eventually was to overshadow the basic foundation by its elaborateness and complexity, the connection to troping was never to disappear completely.

Perhaps this fact of troping as a starting point may serve to explain in part why polyphonic music in the West soon began to lose its improvisational air. Evidently, because of the fixed character of the music on which the added voice or voices were imposed, there was by necessity a certain rigidity that curbed the character of the possible improvisation. No alterations could be made in the given plainchant foundation, for this was determined and immutable by its liturgical nature. The added part, if considered as a note-against-note technique, thereby also carried a certain degree of restriction, limiting the number of notes possible. If we add to this the limitations on the choice of notes enforced by the classification of intervals as perfect and imperfect (understanding that God could not be worshipped by imperfect means), the limits to improvisation were quite narrow. In the final analysis, one might almost conclude that the end product was not really improvised at all, except in the sense that, because of its restrictions of choice to a minimum of possible combinations, it did not need to be written down.

With the growth of interest on the part of composers in polyphony as an artistic expression, these restrictions were gradually relaxed, but the complications that were developed later were still subject to considerations other than just those of beauty of sound. The completed work had also to remain within the philosophical and speculative framework of which music was a part. This could not be achieved to the satisfaction of all parties concerned unless the composer could govern the result and achieve a balance between the two sides, the practical and the speculative. Improvisation alone could not do this, for the singer was not sufficiently trained to understand the speculative necessities, nor could improvisation be called a product of reason except in the most elementary of senses; all too easily the music resulting from uncontrolled improvisation might have sensual beauty of sound but be completely lacking in all that would delight the mind. True polyphony in the highest of senses could not be improvised; it had to be composed, and by one aware of both practical and philosophical requirements.

Without this attention to speculative implications, polyphony could never have advanced beyond its simple beginnings, for its growth depended on more than the technical interest brought to it by the singers in various monasteries. To assume any position of importance within the liturgy and thereby receive the attention of musicians, it had to be accepted by theologians and philosophers within the speculative framework of which monophony had for so long been a part. Such an acceptance was not long in coming, for discussion of the place of polyphony in music as part of the *quadrivium* began in the ninth century, the same century that produced the first technical descriptions.

The first philosopher to speak of polyphony as a speculative element is Johannes Scotus Erigena, master of the court school under Charles the Bald of France. Erigena's *De divisione naturae (Concerning the division of nature)*, from about 876, not only gives a sketchy description of organum as a technique, but also remarks that polyphony suggests the otherwise inexpressible beauty of the universe. Musical harmony in terms of polyphony is thus a representative of cosmic harmony, the music of the spheres, and *musica mundana*. Its beauty is the direct result of the contrast of various proportions in simultaneous sounds, not in consecutive order as in monophony. This beauty, perceptible by reason alone, is, as always, superior to that which comes from the simple sensual pleasure aroused by the physical impact of the sounds. Evidently, the overall concept stems from Boethius, not altered but extended; what is new is the entry of polyphony into the scheme and its assumption of an important place therein.

This definition of the role of polyphony in speculation as outlined by Erigena was amplified by later generations of philosophers. The major clarification made by later writers is the relationship between monophony and polyphony. With the passing of time and the growing importance of polyphony as the major musical technique, there was more and more a tendency to regard monophony as an introductory branch of music, useful to teach fundamentals such as intervals and simple notation. Polyphony was a second stage, of greater importance in both musical and philosophical meanings. The *Declaratio musicae disciplinae* (*Declaration of the discipline of music*) by Ugolino of Orvieto (1375?–1455?) shows this development clearly; in Book II of this work, Ugolino states that, although there is delight in plainchant or *nuda musica* (the name itself suggests a classification) for both the ear and the mind, it is not of the same high degree as in counterpoint. In monophonic music, one does not hear the many intervals in proportion as they resound in polyphony, but only one note after another. Counterpoint allows the reason to judge those elements that cannot be found in monophony, consonance and dissonance. As a typical viewpoint from the close of the Middle Ages and from one of the last medieval theorists, Ugolino's reactions summarize the attitude of the whole period. The relation to the views of Erigena is clear, for Ugolino's position is inherent in the work of the older man.

## THEORETICAL SOURCES

The earliest examples of notated polyphony that we have appear in a treatise of the tenth century, the *Musica enchiriadis* (*Musical manual*), once supposed to be by Hucbald (840–930), but now believed to be by Otger de Laon and written at Valenciennes. Two types of organum are described, the first based on the succession of certain fixed intervals, with or without doubling at the octave, the second, freer in style, where the opening and closing portions are not restricted to one interval. In performing the first type, the given plainchant melody or *vox principalis* is duplicated below at the distance of either a perfect fifth or perfect fourth, producing the *vox organalis;* of importance is the use of intervals in accord with their place in the speculative scheme, for all other intervals were dissonances or imperfect. Once these two lines were achieved, either or both could be duplicated an octave higher, giving composite organum in three or four voices (Example 5-1).

**EXAMPLE 5-1.**

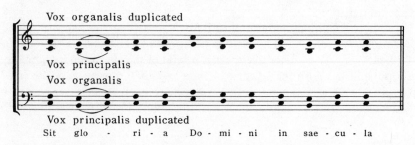

Vox organalis duplicated

Vox principalis
Vox organalis

Vox principalis duplicated
Sit     glo  -  ri - a   Do - mi - ni    in   sae - cu - la

It is evident that occasional problems might well arise in such a duplication at a strict distance, for unless some kind of alteration by inserted accidentals was made, there would be moments when one was obliged to sing a tritone (the augmented fourth or diminished fifth) instead of the proper perfect interval; if the *vox principalis,* for example, were to sing d e f, a *vox organalis* at the fifth below would require G A B, producing the forbidden tritone, the "devil in music" as it was called by medieval musicians. To avoid this, the *Musica enchiriadis* suggests a free organum, with the two voices beginning on the same tone, one of them rising to the interval of a fourth, then both proceeding in parallel motion until near the end, with a close on the unison; an even freer type may be used, with an occasional shift to other intervals within the phrase, depending on the nature of the given plainchant and the necessity for avoiding the tritone (Example 5-2).

**EXAMPLE 5-2.**

In Example 5-2, the difficulties of placing a consecutive series of perfect fourths below the *vox principalis* are apparent, for the tritone would appear at each b. By using unisons, seconds, thirds, and fifths, the clash is avoided and, what is more important, a certain freedom is acquired by the added voice—a freedom, however, more apparent than real, since choices of intervals to be used were not made at the will of the singer, but were determined by the inability to follow normal procedures. Free organum was thus to be used only when strict organum was impossible.

By the beginning of the eleventh century, the relative position of the two styles was no longer the same, for strict parallel organum was of much less interest and of less artistic meaning. Clear evidence of this shift is found in the *Micrologus* of Guido of Arezzo, perhaps the most influential of all medieval treatises, to judge from the number of copies still in existence, the many areas from which they come, and the long period over which they were prepared. Within the *Micrologus,* Guido makes it clear that he prefers the free style because it allows the use of more different intervals in the completed organum. The perfect fourth is the primary interval, with the major and minor thirds and the major second as other possibilities; the perfect fifth and the minor second are not permitted, as they are felt by Guido to be harsh. Other intervals are not mentioned, perhaps because Guido feels that there is no question of their possible employment. The *Micrologus* defines the four usable intervals as "concords" (*concordia*) and the added voice as "diaphony" (*diaphonia*).

In his discussion, Guido grades chants by their suitability for the application of an organal voice, the classification set by the mode of the basic plainchant. The lowest level is held by chants in Modes III and IV, which use the strict manner. Here, the diaphonic voice proceeds at a perfect fourth below the given chant, in the same manner as prescribed in the *Musica enchiriadis*. With Guido's distaste for the perfect fifth, there is here no mention of organum at that interval. The two-voiced organum arrived at by parallel motion is called "hard" (*durum*). As before, the number of voices may be expanded by duplication of the *vox organalis* at the upper octave; no mention is made of duplication of the *vox principalis* in the same way.

Organum in a free style, labeled as "soft" (*molle*), is divided into two types. The simpler is that made by adding a diaphonic line to melodies in Modes I and II. With these chants, one may use not only the perfect fourth but also the major second and minor third. The use of these last two intervals is not common, however, and, for this reason, Guido makes it plain that he much prefers the more complicated type, based on melodies in Modes V through VIII. Organum on chants in these modes frequently includes the major second and major third, again in combination with the perfect fourth. To Guido, this last type is smoother and thus best.

A principal feature of Guido's further discussion is his series of remarks on the *occursus* or "coming together," found at the end of free organum in the second manner. Here, the close of organum is the unison, reached from a penultimate major second or major third (never minor): the effect of the occursus is that of a cadence, evidently considered as a more satisfying close than that of the perfect fourth. Certain of Guido's examples begin with a unison, proceeding then to the organal interval; Example 5-3 is a sample of the possible results.

**EXAMPLE 5-3.**

Vox principalis

Vox organalis

Ve - ni ad do-cen-dum    nos        vi - am pru-den-ti - ae.

Although there is no reference within the treatise to the possibility of voice-crossing, certain of the examples show its employment. One of these uses a diaphonic voice of but one tone throughout the piece, an F repeated to every note of the given chant, which moves above and below this drone-like accompaniment. In addition, the last syllable of the chant is melismatic and one may presume that the F was not reiterated at each note of the melisma, but held out as a long tone, as though with a fermata above it (Example 5-4).

EXAMPLE 5-4.

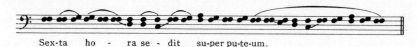

Sex-ta  ho - ra se - dit  su-per pu-te-um.

With the *Micrologus*, the shift from improvisation to composition makes its first timid steps, for it reflects a realization that uniformity of approach and technique is not artistically desirable. Variety is the goal and one cannot give rules that will completely govern every possible situation. Guido's objective in presenting his examples is not that of procedural prescription, but that of showing a few of the many results that can be achieved by the application of a few broad artistic principles.

As the last of the early theoretical sources on organum, the *De musica* (*Concerning music*) by John of Affligem (sometimes referred to as John Cotton) from around 1100 is of paramount interest. Its author was, for many years, presumed to have been an English monk; many later theorists refer to him as such. Modern research has indicated he was probably Flemish in origin, working in a monastery at Affligem. While John's discussion of organum is not extensive, constituting but one chapter of 23 within the *De musica,* it is of importance in showing the further development of free organum and the decline of the strict style; indeed, John does not even mention the latter variety, which suggests that it had long been regarded as of little significance and not worthy of discussion.

The most valuable section of John's description of organum is that insisting on the superior value of contrary motion between the two voices. Parallel motion may occur, but the variety of intervals achieved by contrary motion is to be preferred. Cadences may be made at either the unison or the octave, the choice depending on the nature of the plainchant, that is, whether it closes with an ascending or descending line; unison closes are preferable where possible. John also suggests that the organizing voice may, on occasion, sing two or three notes to one note of the given melody (but he gives no examples of this technique). There are no specific recommendations or directions within the discussion, the emphasis falling more on general principles. Only one short example appears, as a suggested approach and no more, with no implication that this particular excerpt (Example 5-5) is more than but one solution of many.

EXAMPLE 5-5.

Analysis of John's example shows the increased liberty of choice since Guido. Here, one sees all those intervals previously mentioned in the *Micrologus*—the second, third, and fourth—but the perfect fifth and minor seventh appear as well. Significantly, the example begins with a perfect fifth and includes one other, with only one perfect fourth at an unimportant place. Although John says nothing directly on the subject, it is evident that the high place of the perfect fourth as a consonance had begun to pass and that the perfect fifth, originally of inferior status, had started to replace the fourth as the principal consonance after the octave. This trend was to lead, by the fifteenth century, to the paradox that the perfect fourth was theoretically a consonance but, in practice, had all the characteristics of a dissonance and could not be used without special precautions.

During this early period, up to the eleventh century, the employment of counterpoint within the liturgy was not completely determined, except that it was to act as an embellishment and elaboration of chants for those days to be set apart by some particular splendor. From the examples given in the *Musica enchiriadis,* one may deduce that organum was performed by the choir as a whole, for these excerpts (and they are no more than that) are nearly all based on plainchants liturgically assigned to the choir and, with one exception, from the Hours. This hypothesis is not destroyed by the information from the treatises of Guido and John. Most of the examples given in the *Micrologus* are choral chants, although, as in the *Musica enchiriadis,* one passage from a Sequence is included. The single example from the *De musica* is an Antiphon, a Benedictine chant, in which the whole chant, both the solo and choral sections, is in organum.

Up to this point, all of our information comes from monastic treatises, and the written examples we have are part of these works. Taken as a group, these treatises suggest the following conclusions: 1) Organum was originally peculiar to monastery churches, used most often in the chants more usual there, those of the Hours being of particular importance; 2) within the monastery, organum was performed chorally, with many singers on a part; 3) organum was an improvised technique, not needing written form because of the rather limited possibilities set by both the theoretical rules and the practical difficulties of choral improvisation; 4) as seen in the problems of the perfect fourth and its classification as a consonance, speculative theory had begun to find opposition in the face of practical experience.

## PRACTICAL SOURCES

With the later eleventh century, practical musical sources—manuscripts containing composed organum—began to appear, principally in France and England. The contents of these volumes, together with later theoretical treatises, indicate that the era of composed organum had begun and that the place of polyphony within the liturgy was no longer restricted to primarily monastic chants. Most of our sources now show greater ties to the cathedral than to the monastery and indicate that the great innovations in polyphonic technique no longer stem from the cloister but from choir schools attached to public churches. Even the theoretical works show something of this, for, although many continue to be produced by regular clergy, more and more of them come from outside clerical centers; of these, one describing twelfth-century practice is written in French, implying strongly the new atmosphere. If written for the usual audience of preceding times, it would have been in Latin.

The major changes in the function of polyphony that came with the eleventh century are tied to two new developments. The first of these is the change from a choral to a soloistic repertoire. The insertion of counterpoint within the liturgy is now limited to those passages prescribed for performance by a cantor, not those for the choir. Thus no chant was completely set in organum; choral plainchant now alternated with polyphony. In addition, when counterpoint was added to solo sections of the chant, it continued to be performed by soloists, thereby retaining the soloist-choir dichotomy originally in liturgical monophony. The restriction of polyphony to solo sections, however, did not rest alone on the liturgical shape of the music because, whether improvised or composed, the new organum was of such technical difficulty that it required greater skill and training. The average choir member was not able to cope with the new developments. The soloists, on the other hand, were specially selected and musically educated products of the *schola cantorum;* it was for them that many of the treatises of the time were prepared, treatises emphasizing the new techniques to the detriment of the older speculative elements.

Just as certain poets and musicians of the eleventh and twelfth centuries had used the Alleluia as the springboard for their own extensions, so did composers of the same period begin their experiments with the new organum in the same way. In the eleventh century, it was already the custom at Chartres to use organum in the Alleluia chants for Epiphany, Easter Day, the week following Easter, the Feast of the Assumption, the Feast of St. Augustine, and the Feast of St. Martin: all these days were of sufficient importance to require polyphony as a distinguishing feature. Thirteen eleventh-century Alleluia settings are found inserted into two ninth-century manuscripts at Chartres, with five in notation sufficiently clear to be deciphered today. Example 5-6 is the opening of the Verse to the Alleluia for Easter (*LU*, 786).

**EXAMPLE 5-6.**

The extreme freedom used by the composer in his choice of intervals is immediately apparent. Not only are all the previously mentioned intervals employed, but there is even a major sixth on the penultimate note. The perfect fourth is still a preferred interval, but a surprising succession of three thirds appears where one might have expected fourths. The use of a cadential unison or octave at the end of each word is not to be overlooked, nor is the beginning of each on a perfect fourth. Finally, it is clear that the composer's goal in his added voice was not one of providing a secondary musical line against which to set off the beauty of the given chant; his hope was rather to provide a second melody of the same quality as the *vox principalis*, of the same artistic meaning as the fundamental chant. Contrary motion, parallel motion, free choice of intervals, clear cadences—all enter into the achievement of this goal.

The largest source of eleventh-century organum is one of the two manuscripts known collectively as the *Winchester Tropers*, containing over 150 two-voice compositions. Unfortunately, the notation is at present undecipherable and little can be said specifically about the technique employed, except that there is evidence of crossing voices and contrary motion. In general, however, the *vox principalis* is below the *vox organalis*, a position that it was to occupy thenceforth. With this change of position, the ornamenting voice takes on an importance that indicates something of the place of the new organum; the process that we saw already beginning in the Chartres manuscript, the raising of the added line from a position of support to one of equality, is later carried forward to a new point of departure, wherein this new material will become of greater artistic interest than the given chant on which it is superimposed. While this development is still embryonic in the *Winchester Tropers* (and not wholly clear because of notational difficulties), it is a first step in the chain of events that led to the magnificent achievements of the thirteenth century, the overfulfillment of the liturgical function by the demands of artistic expression and the submergence of functional plainchant under a contrapuntal superstructure.

In spite of the English provenance of the *Winchester Tropers*, the basic source of the organum style is probably French, from the North, possibly Fleury. The monophonic repertoire within the sources reflects a strong influence of that center and it is known that connections between England and the Continent were close; William the Conqueror had requested the aid of French monks in the reform of monastic music and, in at least one case, brought over a French monk to take charge of an English monastery, that at Glastonbury. The organal repertoire is perhaps not all French, but, in view of the origins of the monophonic material, it seems logical to assume that the models for its creation came from France; a later source, a table of contents of a now lost manuscript of the twelfth century, names a W[illiam?] of Winchester as a composer of organum, indicating the growth of a native production, not imported.

The contents of the organal sections show clearly the effort to provide material for the general service of the most important days—Christmas, Easter, and Epiphany, among others. Twelve Kyries and eight Glorias, all troped, are set, indicating a turn to the Ordinary of the Mass, although there are no organa to either the Sanctus or Agnus; the insecure liturgical place of the Credo accounts for its noninclusion. The largest part of the collection consists of 73 Alleluia-Tract settings, covering the liturgical year, followed in number by 51 Responsories; other elements include the Invitatory (3), processional Antiphon (3), Sequence (12), and Easter Introit Trope from the early liturgical drama (3). Evidently, the same urge that led to a systematic provision of monophony in the early Church was at work here, but now with the use of polyphony; though the results are incomplete, the plan is clear.

In the late eleventh and early twelfth centuries, the major role in the development or organum belongs to the monastery of St. Martial at Limoges, a center already mentioned in our discussion of the history of the troubadour movement. Under a succession of gifted abbots, St. Martial became a leading artistic center in almost every area including poetry, fine arts, and music; at the beginning of the twelfth century, its library was the second largest of any monastery in France.

Among the twenty-three volumes known collectively as the *St. Martial Tropers*, there are four manuscripts, three in Paris and one in London, containing organa. These include 76 polyphonic items in all, with some duplications from one source to another. As in the *Winchester Tropers,* one manuscript, the oldest (from the late eleventh century), presents its five organa in a notational guise that does not allow transcription into modern form with complete security. The notation used in the other three (from the middle of the twelfth century) is more certain, although there are difficulties in understanding the relations between groups of notes occurring simultaneously in the given melody and its added line; even though many scholars have assumed a rhythmic performance like that in secular melodies of the same time, the notation itself contains no indications of such a possibility.

The repertoire within these four manuscripts, both monophonic and polyphonic, shows the high place given to what we have labeled accretions to the liturgy. There is heavy emphasis on the Sequence, troped parts of the Mass Ordinary (the Kyrie, Sanctus, and Agnus), as well as tropings of the Proper (the Gradual and Epistles). Conductus make up a large part of the repertoire, not only some composed as processionals but also others written for special occasions, such as a New Year's greeting of the choir to its cantor. There is even a conductus of censure, a condemnation of evil customs of the day, a rarity at the time. The liturgical drama is not overlooked, and there are numerous tropes on the Benedicamus Domino, as well as a handful of items that also appear in the *Carmina Burana.* Although not all these types are found in the polyphonic works, the organa reflect this emphasis on the artistic derivations of the liturgy; only one item, a Benedicamus, appears in a pure form, without trope.

The major contribution of the School of St. Martial was the solution of the problem of organal counterpoint, setting up the basis on which the future development of polyphonic techniques was to build. We have already noted John of Affligem's reference to the possibility of using two or three notes in the *vox organalis* to one in the *vox principalis.* Composers of St. Martial, amplifying this simple procedure, began to take the given chant and stretch its length many times, while adding a *duplum,* the now customary name for the newly composed voice, of many notes above it; melismata of twenty notes above a held tone are not uncommon. This new method, referred to as *organum* style by the theorists of the time, amounts to a suppression of the musical nature of the original plainchant in favor of the artistic possibilities inherent in the new emphasis on the duplum. The term used for the given chant foundation reflects this new attitude, for it was no longer called the *vox principalis,* but the *tenor,* its name deriving from "tenere" ("to hold out"); its designation was no longer taken from its liturgical place, but was based on its artistic and technical function. In its new situation, it was not the principal voice, for that position was now held by the added voice or voices.

Together with organum style, the older note-against-note technique, now known as *discantus* style, continued. Unlike the approach found in the Chartres manuscript, where the goal was to imitate the characteristics of chant in the added voice, the discantus of St. Martial followed the lead of organum style in differentiating between the tenor and the discantus; it was guided more by the technical need for voice leading, with consonances at appropriate points. In addition, it was not always necessary to maintain a strict note-against-note relation. Short units of two and three notes might be introduced in the duplum against one in the tenor, thus providing artistic variety. Both styles, organum and discantus, might appear in the same work, most frequently in the troped Benedicamus chants. Conductus, because of its essentially syllabic character, was normally set in discantus style. We append here two short examples of the styles, the first in organum (Example 5-7), the second in elaborated discantus (Example 5-8).

**EXAMPLE 5-7.**

Tenor

Be -        ne -                    di-camus

**EXAMPLE 5-8.**

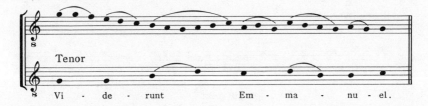

Tenor

Vi  -  de  -  runt        Em  -  ma  -  nu  -  el.

Whether or not the practices of St. Martial were of great influence on the flowering of polyphony at Notre Dame in Paris during the following century is a still unsolved problem. Even though there are many evidences of common approach, it is not possible to say definitely that the great School of Notre Dame was a direct outgrowth of that of St. Martial; no work in the St. Martial repertoire appears in that of Notre Dame. A more probable influence of St. Martial was that on Spain and, indirectly, on England.

The Spanish relationship to St. Martial is suggested by the Codex Calixtinus from Santiago de Compostella, a manuscript from around 1140 containing twenty organa in addition to many monophonic works. It was a product of the importance of Compostella as a center for pilgrimage; it was believed that St. James the Apostle had died there and bones reputed to be his were exposed for veneration within the Cathedral. Visitors from all over Europe, particularly from France, were numerous. This is reflected in the manuscript, for many pieces are prefaced by the names of French ecclesiastical dignitaries, implying that these men may well have been the composers; however, in all probability, the names were added later for purposes of prestige. The style of the polyphonic pieces is clearly relatable to the practices of St. Martial, as is the liturgical repertoire generally. The most interesting feature of the manuscript is the presence of what is believed to be the oldest piece of real three-voice organum as distinguished from that achieved by voice duplication; it is, typically enough, a troped Benedicamus.

As a sample of the style, we present a section of a troped two-voice Benedicamus from Compostella (Example 5-9); only the first and last of the four strophes are given.

EXAMPLE 5-9.

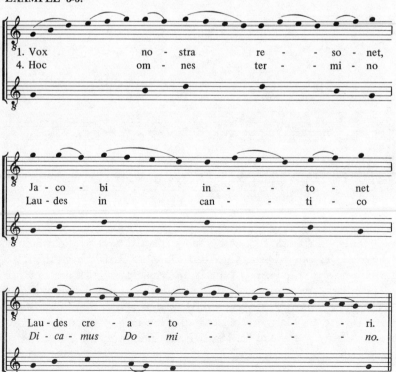

It is particularly interesting to notice the different counterpoint for the first two lines, for the given melody in the tenor is the same for both. The opening of the first line is appropriately more elaborate, for it sets the scene, so to speak, for what is to follow. At the end, as at the beginning, there is an elaborate extension, obviously to bring the line to . a satisfying close. There is, as one might expect, a reliance on formulae, on use of somewhat the same kind of solution for similar situations. The emphasis on contrary motion as a guiding principle is also important, for it gives individuality to the added line and effectively sets it off against the given tenor.

In view of the presence of many English pilgrims at Compostella, one may presume that the nine organa found in a twelfth-century source now in Cambridge were derived through Spanish contact, if not directly. In style they follow the continental model closely, using the techniques developed at St. Martial. The repertoire is much the same, relying heavily upon various troped elements and conductus.

In summary, the latter part of the twelfth century saw the establishment of polyphony as a major force within the music of the church. While its rhythmic elements were not yet clearly defined—a task to be taken up by the musicians of Paris and, in particular, Notre Dame—the basic understanding of the relation of the newly composed material to its plainchant foundation had been firmly established. A definition of style had been made and an exploration of its artistic possibilities had been started. There had also been a final definition of polyphony as a soloistic art, relying on the trained musician and educated specialist. Most important, however, was the new place of plainchant, no longer the center of musical interest, but solely the starting point for the new contrapuntal structures.

To some extent, polyphony in the late twelfth century had begun its attack upon the liturgical character of music, for, with its introduction and its elaboration, the basic function of plainchant had been altered. It might be overstatement to say that polyphony had destroyed the function of music within the Church—a close relationship among the text, the liturgical act, and the music—but it may be suggested that the process had begun. While the ostensible purpose for the introduction of organum had been the enhancement of the services, it is evident that composers were already beginning to go far beyond this point, driven on by their artistic urge for expression. While the Church did not then recognize the danger and in fact encouraged the new music in every way, it was not to be long until complaints were registered over what intelligent ecclesiastics could see was a usurpation. By the end of the thirteenth century, the consequences of what had been developed by St. Martial would be understood as the dangers to liturgy that they were.

## BIBLIOGRAPHICAL NOTES

Most of the sources connected with the early history of polyphony have been mentioned previously. Most research in this area has been done by German scholars, men such as Jacques Handschin and Friedrich Ludwig, whose works have not been translated into English. For the student who can read German, the best survey is that given by Ludwig in Guido Adler's *Handbuch der Musikgeschichte* (Berlin: Max Hesses Verlag, 1930). The latest work to treat the subject is Max Lütolf, *Mehrstimmige Ordinarium Missae-Sätze*, 2 vols. (Bern: Paul Haupt, 1970); there are a number of facsimiles at the end of the first volume, the second volume then giving a large number of transcriptions, many of them coming from the early period of polyphonic development. The bibliography at the end of the first volume is exhaustive; however, consult Gordon A. Anderson's review of this work in *Musical Quarterly*, LVII (1971). Theodore Karp's "St. Martial and Santiago de Compostela: An Analytical Speculation," *Acta Musicologica*, XXXIX (1967), must be mentioned as a major contribution in English. There is also much information in Frank Ll. Harrison, *Music in Medieval Britain* (London: Routledge and Kegan Paul, 1958), although the approach is geographically limited.

# SIX

# THE SCHOOL OF NOTRE DAME

To the middle of the twelfth century, the history of polyphony is difficult to trace with any real continuity. No one area can be singled out as that of primary leadership and guidance, for we have no evidence of any sequence of interrelationships in polyphony's development and spread through Europe. Those who describe early polyphony, the theorists, come from all parts of the continent and are concerned with local practice. The purely musical sources, those including compositions, seem not to have been known outside the circumscribed area for which they were originally prepared. In the case of St. Martial, a degree of influence on Spain and England has been suggested, but there is no secure evidence except on stylistic grounds; there is no bit of repertoire that appears in sources coming from other places, either at the same time or later. Polyphony thus appears to have grown in various centers and at various times, without cross-connections from one locality to another. Solutions to musical and artistic problems posed by organum were resolved in restricted areas; they do not seem to have been carried over into the music of other centers. To this point, then, polyphony can be considered as but a provincial art and little more.

With the mid-twelfth century, the first truly universal musical leadership makes its appearance. The rise of a school of composition centered in Paris and, in particular, at the Cathedral of Notre Dame is the beginning of the henceforth normal domination of musical style and technique by representatives of one area. Not only did the procedures, as worked out by musicians from this center, become the standard for those from others, but their specific works were copied again and again into non-Parisian sources, in places as distant as Scotland and Spain. A hundred years after their composition certain works were still part of a living repertoire, for they were still being copied for performance purposes.

Why this should have come about may, in part, be explained by the position of Paris itself during the latter half of the twelfth and early thirteenth centuries. As an education center, Paris then had no equal, for the University of Paris, although recognized only around 1173, had grown to a position of scholastic preeminence. Such teachers as St. Bernard of Clairvaux (1090–1153), Peter Abelard (1079–1142), John of Salisbury (d. 1180) and Peter Lombard (d. 1163) had early attracted the best minds of all Europe; a contemporary remarked, "The Italians have the Papacy, the Germans the Empire; the French have Education." The brillance of the University alone has been enough to justify the naming of this period by some historians as the "Renaissance" of the twelfth cenutry.

The University, however, was not all that made Paris a leading city, for the political situation in France had been stabilized under Louis VI (1081–1137) and Louis VII (1119–1180). With the able counsel of Suger (1081?–1151), the Abbot of St. Denis, both kings were able to concentrate power in their own hands and to make Paris, their capital, the chief city of France. It was during their reigns that the major Gothic monuments of Paris were started; the Church of St. Denis (begun 1136) and the new Cathedral of Notre Dame (begun 1163) are but two of the great achievements. With Philippe Augustus (1165–1223), the advances made under the two earlier kings were continued. During his rule, Paris became the cultural center of all Europe, attracting students and visitors from all parts of the continent.

It was in this climate that the musical advances made by Notre Dame musicians began. There had long been a choir school attached to the Cathedral; Peter Lombard, while Biship of Paris, had done much to support it and to make it an integral part of the University. John of Salisbury, from his own account, attended performances of the choir at Notre Dame and, to judge by his description, heard it in the polyphony for which it was to become famous. Other visitors also report on it and make it evident that it was a major attraction of the city. With this school as a model, other churches of Paris began to emulate Notre Dame, so that, by the beginning of the thirteenth century, what we now call the Notre Dame repertoire is, in reality, not only that of the Cathedral but many other churches as well; a better term for the period might well be that of the School of Ile-de-France, although it does not suggest the primacy of Notre Dame as a generating force.

## THE NOTATION OF RHYTHM

In previous discussion of both monophony and polyphony, the peculiar difficulties over the nature and employment of rhythm have been mentioned. While we may be fairly certain that some form of rhythmic differentiation between notes existed in performance, the notation of the music itself offers no clear indications what was done. The rhythmic transcriptions that have been made have, in general, been based on the nature of the text or on the application of certain basic rhythmic patterns to the notes; the results cannot be guaranteed. Even in those cases where a rhythmic interpretation may be founded on some few notational variations, as in certain St. Martial works, there are never enough of them to make the results positive.

It is in this area that Notre Dame made one of its major technical contributions, a system whereby the performer would have a guide to the rhythmic characteristics of a composition. This system, whose foundations were laid by Leonin, the first great Notre Dame composer and master of its choir around 1160, is based on a set of six basic rhythmic patterns known as the rhythmic modes. These patterns, indicated by the notation, were to be applied by the performer in a more or less fixed manner to the melody. In essence, the rhythmic modes are various arrangements of long and short values, corresponding to various poetic meters; indeed, it is now believed that the major inspiration for this method was derived by Leonin from his study of St. Augustine's *De musica,* a treatise on metrics. These six patterns of *longae* and *breves* (the Latin terms for long and short notes) are shown in Example 6-1.

The performer's understanding of the proper pattern to be applied was gained from inspection of the groupings of the notes in the notation. Plainchant had long used figures that placed into one group two or more notes, but had normally used these without great plan or purpose, except to indicate, in a general way, those groups to be sung to the same syllable. Leonin, on the other hand, employed these groups, now called ligatures,

**EXAMPLE 6-1.**

to direct the performer to the correct rhythmic mode. If, for example, the particular melody was to be performed in the first mode, the ligatures were written in such a way to give a grouped pattern of a three-note ligature at the beginning followed by a series of twos; second mode was indicated by the reverse, i.e. a series of two-note ligatures followed by one of threes. The other modes also had their own individual patterns, so that identification would, as much as possible, be certain. To show the system on its simplest levels, we give in Example 6-2 short phrases in each of the six rhythmic modes, followed by their transcription into modern notation (the brackets above the notes in transcription indicate the original ligatures).

**EXAMPLE 6-2.**

Variations within the individual patterns could be made in various ways—by adding an extra note to a ligature, by taking the notes of ligatures and writing them as separate or simple notes (*simplices*), or by adding a tail up or down (*plica*: indicated in transcription by a slash through the stem of the note) to a *simplex* or to the last note of a ligature.

In this way, the various modes might be provided with notes longer than normally found (*extensio modi*) or with short notes gotten by dividing a normal note into two smaller parts (*fractio modi*). The phrase in Example 6-3, with transcription, illustrates the variety possible within the first mode; similar variety is obtainable in the other five.

EXAMPLE 6-3.

In addition, the composer was not limited to one rhythmic mode throughout a composition, for shifts from one to another were possible, provided that a rest of some kind intervened. A piece might begin in the first mode, and, at the conclusion of a section, marked by the presence of a rest, begin anew in second mode.

Although the fundamental characteristics of modal notation are comparatively simple, in actual practice there are many problems in determining exactly how a particular passage is to be transcribed. With the possibilities of variation outlined above, it is often difficult to determine exactly what mode is to be used, and, even if the overall mode is fairly clear, one frequently has difficulty in determining whether one is to use procedures based on *fractio* or *extensio*. This is particularly true of organa for two voices, where the length of the tenor is not exact and the amount of space to be filled by the duplum is not certain. For these reasons, it is the custom of the modern editor to include the brackets for ligatures and the slashed notes for plicas, so that the user may see just how the interpretation has been derived. Two editors may and often do make different interpretations of the same passage, both well-founded and logical, but fitting the patterns into different modes.

Our knowledge of the workings of this system is, like that for earlier practice, based mainly on the writings of various theorists who describe more or less clearly the methods used. One of the most useful volumes for the study of modal notation (and later notation as well) is a compendium prepared by a Bohemian priest, Jerome of Moravia, around 1272. Jerome seems to have been a teacher in the Dominican cloister of St. Jacques in Paris, working within the framework of the University. His compilation is of particular value, since it not only reveals the contents of a typical medieval university course in music but also gives in chronological order four treatises by other authors—treatises that, by their contents, give an overall history of the advances made and techniques of notation used at various periods. The earliest of the four describes practices of the late twelfth cenutry; the latest, procedures from Jerome's own times.

A second source of value is a treatise written by an anonymous Englishman around 1280. From internal evidence, he was a student at the University of Paris and was interested not only in the theory of music but also in its practice. It is through information given by him that we know something of the achievements of Leonin; no other sources name him or discuss his work. This English student is usually referred to as Anonymous IV, for his treatise was first printed in a modern version around the mid-nineteenth century by the French scholar, Edmond de Coussemaker, as the fourth in a series of anonymous treatises.

## SOURCES

In comparison with the paucity of musical sources for the early history of polyphony, the era using modal notation is well supplied. In addition to three large sources, there are many smaller ones, all containing items from the great repertoire developed by the early School of Notre Dame and indicating by their reliance upon that repertoire the immense influence spreading out from Paris. The oldest of the three major sources is that found today in Wolfenbüttel at the Herzogliche Bibliothek under the call number 677. Although probably prepared in St. Andrews, Scotland, in the fourteenth century, it seems closest to Leonin and his time, in spite of its comparatively late date; in the literature it is referred to as W¹. A second manuscript, from France of the thirteenth or fourteenth centuries, is also preserved in the same library; its call number is 1206 and it is given the short reference W². The third major source is a French manuscript in Florence, Biblioteca Medicea-Laurenziana, Pluteus 29.1; the word "Pluteus" here refers to the position of the book on a particular shelf in a specific place in the library. Pluteus 29.1 dates from between 1245 and 1255 and, in the scholarly literature, has the *siglum* (identifying abbreviation) F. All three of the above sources are fairly extensive and include, in addition to the material in modal notation, much music of later date, from a time when notational methods had begun to change.

Of the subsidiary manuscripts, the most inclusive is that found today in Madrid, Biblioteca Nacional, with the call number 20468 and reference as Ma; it is of Spanish provenance and is from the fourteenth century. Other important sources are preserved in libraries in Munich, London, and Paris, but, although they are of value in the study of the period, their contents are generally not as extensive in either number or variety as those of the three manuscripts cited first.

## THE WORK OF LEONIN

In writing of the musical situation at Paris, Anonymous IV, the English student, states that ". . . And note that Master Leonin . . . was the best composer of organa, a man who composed a great book [*Magnus Liber*] of organum based on the Graduale and Antiphonale, for the enlargement of the divine service. . . ." Within this statement lies the key to Leonin's greatness, for it was he who began the systematic expansion of the new organum into the whole of the repertoire. In its reconstructed form, based on the three main manuscripts and what is probably the oldest version, the *Magnus Liber* includes 13 pieces for the Hours and 33 works for the Mass. Both sections begin with works for Christmas and continue into the liturgical year, providing not only items for the major feast days but also works for various other occasions. The emphasis in the material for the Hours is placed on various Processional Responsories, while that in the Mass stresses the Gradual and Alleluia, the two chants already singled out as especially suitable for polyphonic treatment by their soloistic character.

All of the works in the *Magnus Liber* are for two voices and reflect the division into the two styles previously described, organum and discantus. Only those portions of the chant liturgically designed for solo performance by the cantor are set polyphonically; the choral parts are to be sung in plainchant as before. Thus, these works begin with a polyphonic movement and are then interrupted by the plainchant areas, to return again to polyphony wherever a solo section begins again. The commencement of each polyphonic section is in organum style, with the tenor held out under a long melismatic flourish by the duplum; this last, in the works of Leonin, is always in the first rhythmic mode, for he used no other in the dupla of his works. Within the body of the organum, there are contrasting sections in discantus style, most often corresponding to those places where the basic plainchant is melismatic. Here, the duplum does not fall into the classification of discantus in the manner defined by St. Martial, that is, with note against note; instead, it continues its elaborations around the first mode, while the tenor proceeds in a series of notes of equal rhythmic value, in units occupying one or two beats of the basic pulse.

In this practice Leonin added a new way of defining organum and discantus, not in terms of the number of notes against the tenor but in terms of the rhythmic structure of the tenor. For Leonin, organum style is that in which the tenor is unmeasured, this is, without a fixed length and held to a point of agreement in its close with the ornamented duplum. Discantus style, on the other hand, is that in which the tenor is measured, that is, where its note-lengths may be defined in small rhythmic units. In both cases, the duplum is the same, written basically in the first rhythmic mode and proceeding in this manner throughout the work. To make the coincidence of tenor and duplum clear, the music within the sources is notated in score, with the duplum above the tenor; thus, the performers have little difficulty in achieving a correspondence between the two voices.

Within the sections or *clausulae* of organa, Leonin sets off major cadential points by coming to rest on either the octave, unison, or perfect fifth. There are also points of lesser cadence or places where both voices have simultaneous rests. In these places, other intervals may appear, such as the perfect fourth or the major third; these are, however, quite rare, for Leonin maintains the primacy of the three perfect intervals mentioned as those best for points of rest. Beginnings of organa are often ornamented with an accented appoggiatura from a major or minor seventh leading into the octave; this type of opening acts as a flourish to catch attention. Certain organa also see this used at internal cadences, as a way of emphasis. As to beginnings after cadences, Leonin is not as strict in his choice of intervals as at the cadences proper; the perfect fourth appears frequently here, together with the third and sixth, the latter normally as an accented appoggiatura into the fifth.

All of these points may be seen in Example 6-4, the opening of the Verse, "Audi filia," from the Gradual, "Propter veritatem," for August 15, the Assumption of the Blessed Virgin Mary.

With Leonin's work, the process of elimination of the melodic function of the tenor was complete. With its arrangement of voices and the rhythmically organized character of the duplum, Leonin's organum had obscured the original purpose of the chant to such a point that it was now important only as a starting point for the addition of the second voice. By its subservience to the rhythmic mode, the duplum also made clean its break with the past, for it is clear that Leonin's goal was far different from that of the composer of the earlier works in the Chartres manuscript; there is no desire to imitate the outlines of chant in the added duplum. Indeed, inspection of many organa from the *Magnus Liber* shows again and again the presence of melodic formulae that suggest certain musical concepts peculiar to this kind of musical work and without relation to others; many of these melodic patterns are triadic, something not heard in chant melodies.

Later composers added to the *Magnus Liber*, almost doubling it in size. Their additions can usually be identified by the presence of modes other than the first, as well as by more highly organized tenor patterns. As with Leonin, their aim was the introduction of polyphony into those services of higher importance and the provision of organa for the full

**EXAMPLE 6-4.**

liturgical year. In Example 6-5, we give another setting of the same text, obviously composed after Leonin because of its use of third mode in the duplum, yet still influenced by the same stylistic approach.

**EXAMPLE 6-5.** Reprinted by permission of the Yale University Press from *The Rhythm of Twelfth Century Polyphony,* by William G. Waite. Copyright 1954 by Yale University Press.

While these expansions of technique show the exploitation of the common foundation to a new artistic complexity, one must never forget that the original plan was Leonin's and that the inspiration was his. There can be no doubt that he must be considered one of the great musical minds in the history of Western music.

## THE WORK OF PEROTIN

The quotation from Anonymous IV given above continues: "And it [the *Magnus Liber*] was in use up to the time of Perotin the Great, who abbreviated it and made many better clausulae or points [sections in counterpoint], since he was the best composer of discantus and better than Leonin was. . . ." From these remarks, it is clear that one of Perotin's major accomplishments was the revision of Leonin's work, substituting clausulae in discantus style for those originally written in organum style and shortening older sections in discantus by providing newer ones.

That there was a need for this kind of curtailment is obvious, since the length of the original chant, by its performance in the extended values required in organum style, had become intolerable. Although the chants set had been those of primarily musical interest, without associated liturgical acts, there was evidently a feeling that, by their now increased length, a certain liturgical balance had been disturbed and that equilibrium could only be restored by reducing the time consumed. There was no question of removing polyphony, by now well established and approved; nor was there the possibility of cutting the length of the basic chant by removal of some of its notes. The solution was then one of condensation of the duplum by pruning it of excessive elaboration.

These substitute clausulae are found in abundance in all three of our main sources, where they are identified by the words or syllables of the material they are designed to replace. For example, W[1] includes four of these substitute clausulae with the one syllable, "Go." These were composed to replace music in the organum, "Benedicta. Vir*go* dei genitrix." Why so many substitute clausulae have been provided for chants that would be, because of their place in the Proper, performed but once a year has not yet been clarified; F alone contains over 450 of these substitutes, not only in discantus style but also in recomposed organum, enough to provide alternatives for each basic organum of the *Magnus Liber* many times over.

As a sample of the process, we give the beginning of a substitute clausula for "Filia" (Example 6-6), to be used as a replacement within the organum of the previous example; this particular clausula is from W[1], where it is the second of two for the same piece.

**EXAMPLE 6-6.**

Fi - (lia)

Perotin's most important development was the extension of the use
of rhythmic modes within the tenor. In the work of Leonin, discantus
sections find the tenor normally in fifth mode; Perotin uses all six modes.
Within the duplum, Leonin had used only the first mode; here too,
Perotin employs all six. The result of Perotin's innovations within the
clausula is that both voices are now of rhythmic interest and that there
is what we might call rhythmic counterpoint. Just as variety had been
previously achieved by the opposition of one voice, the duplum, moving
somewhat rapidly against longer values in the tenor, so now additional
variety could be gained through the application of duplum techniques to
the tenor.

Although, if we are to take the word of Anonymous IV, the eventual goal was the abbreviation of organum, Perotin and his followers
found that excessive shortening by the application of shorter rhythmic
patterns did not allow sufficient scope for musical development. Thus, in
many substitute clausulae, they resorted to repetition of the tenor, either
literally or in new patterns. The "Filia" clausula, whose beginning is
given in Example 6-6, portrays this, for, after the whole chant section on
which the clausula is based is given once in the three-note pattern shown
above, it is repeated in a six-note scheme; the variety achieved by this
altered repetition is evident (see Example 6-7).

EXAMPLE 6-7.

Together with stylistic expansion of two-voice organa through
substitution and recomposition within the work of Leonin, Perotin enlarged the framework of organa by adding one or two more voices to the
contrapuntal web. His two four-voice organa, "Viderunt," the Gradual
for Christmas, and "Sederunt," that for the feast of St. Stephen (December 26), were singled out for special notice by Anonymous IV. "Viderunt"
appears in both W[1] and F as the opening work, with "Sederunt" immediately following, indicating their importance to medieval musicians.
Both works can be dated with some degree of accuracy, for edicts of
Bishop Eude de Sully of Notre Dame indicate that "Viderunt" is of 1198
and "Sederunt" is of the following year. Some edicts specify the use of
three- and four-voice organa in special places in the services, mainly the
Responsories and Benedicamus in Vespers and the Gradual and Alleluia

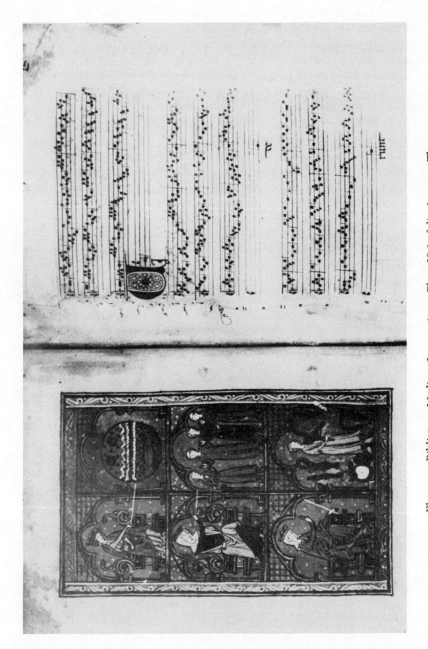

Florence, Biblioteca Mediceea-Laurenziana, Plut. 29.1, folio 1 recto. The music given is the opening of Perotin's organum for the Gradual, "Viderunt," for four voices, to be sung on Christmas Day. The illumination at the left includes a player on the vielle.

in the Mass. Certain others include Matins as suitable for polyphony, with particular feasts singled out for special attention. So far as four-voice organa are concerned, the plan was never completed, for, in addition to the two works of Perotin, only one other has survived, "Mors," from the Alleluia for the Fourth Sunday after Easter.

The style of Perotin's four- and three-voice organa is specifically discussed at some length and with approval by Johannes de Garlandia (1195?–1272?), whose treatise is one of those included in the compendium prepared by Jerome of Moravia. The rules for the ornamenting (*colores*) of the upper voices are three in number, corresponding roughly to the rules for the introduction of ornaments into rhetoric; this is not surprising, for Johannes was a grammarian at the University of Paris. The first manner is the repetition of an initial tone through a fifth or through a sequential pattern; this style is best used in three- and four-voice organa. The second method is a "flowering of the voice" (*florificatio vocis*), the repeating of single notes within a scale-wise progression; according to Johannes, this kind of ornamentation is used most often in secular music. The final manner is the exchange of parts, that is, what one voice sings is taken over by the other; this is employed in almost all kinds of polyphony—organa, conductus, and others. All three manners are given in Example 6-8, taken from those given by Johannes within his treatise.

**EXAMPLE 6-8.**

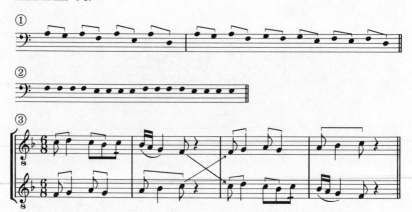

With these works, it is evident that the function of melody is that of generating a motive, which then is to be treated as a formula-like unit. The equality of the upper voices, their occupying the same range, the repetition of melodic formulae from one voice to the other, and the added drone of the tenor lead to an overall impression of monotony, yet intoxicating in the final effect. The composer's ideal is not the presentation

of melody as such, but rather the emphasis on rhythmic patterns that are
supported by melodic movement; these patterns are then organized on a
large skeleton that can be grasped only by feeling the symmetries from
one group of formulae to another; the formula-like nature of the upper
parts is shown by the fact that, when the same tenor note reappears in a
composition, the upper voices often repeat the material originally found
with that note. The opening of Perotin's "Alleluia-Nativitas" (Example
6-9) indicates the general style.

**EXAMPLE 6-9.**

In addition to Perotin's work as composer of substitute clausulae
and three- and four-voice organa, Anonymous IV also cites him as the
author of conductus in one, two, and three voices, giving specific titles in
each category. As we have noted earlier, although the conductus was
originally functionally part of the liturgy, its development was such that
it came to be reflective of the non-liturgical side of clerical activity. In
the thirteenth century, some liturgical connotation is still to be found,
but more and more the emphasis turns to artistic aspects of the music and
to non-liturgical subjects for its poetry. Around the beginning of the century, conductus became the cleric's way of commenting on the events of
the day, the death of a king or bishop, the election of a pope, the accession of a king, or the seizure of a city in war. Conductus was a clerical
art, comparable to that of the troubadour and trouvère in terms of the
music of a defined social stratum.

The most engaging feature of polyphony, as applied to conductus,
was the complete control of the finished product by the creator. Unlike
polyphony composed for liturgical purposes, conductus had no given

melody on which to erect a superstructure, a distinction made clear by all
the theorists of the time. The treatise of Franco of Cologne (fl. 1250), also
part of Jerome of Moravia's compilation, describes the process of getting
the foundation: "Whoever wishes to write conductus should first invent
the most beautiful melody that he can: then he should use it like a tenor
in making discantus." There is no possibility of employing organum style
in writing conductus; this style could only be employed where there was a
cantus prius factus, a piece of chant already present. There is, in conductus, no contrast between the given material and the composed additions as in organum; all is composed, both foundation melody and overall
structure.

The most elaborate variety of conductus is that in which the composer has set his poetic text in a through-composed manner, i.e., with
each strophe receiving new music and with non-texted sections serving
as contrast. These last, called caudae (tails), may appear at the beginning,
between strophes, and at the end of conductus and can be identified by
their lack of poetry below the music. Although these caudae may have
been performed as instrumental interludes, it is also possible that they
were sung, in the manner of a vocalise. On a lower level, there are
many conductus without caudae and with the music repeated for
each succeeding strophe; Anonymous IV suggests that this group was
written for the use of less skilled singers and is of lower artistic merit.

Both in number and in complexity, conductus for two voices pre-
dominate, with approximately 130 preserved examples, as against 60
three-voice works. Within the repertoire for two voices, approximately
half are through-composed, the rest set strophically. Caudae are found in
all but one of the former group and in two-thirds of the strophic settings.
Three-voice conductus does not show this frequency of caudae, and the
few with four voices have no caudae. From these facts, it is evident that
two-voice conductus with caudae are the most artistically significant
types, the centers of the repertoire, to judge from the attention given
them. Indeed, many three-voice conductus found in W$^1$ are modernized
in Ma by dropping the uppermost voice, reducing the texture to two
voices.

The quotation given above from Franco of Cologne makes it clear
that conductus is subject to modal rhythm, for in technique it is a branch
of discantus style. The syllabic character of conductus, however, frequently makes it difficult to determine with accuracy exactly which mode
is to be applied and in what way. The problem is caused by the fact that
the ligature patterns that indicate the mode are by necessity broken up;
the syllabic nature of the poetry and its being set with one to four notes
to the syllable do not allow for an extended series of ligatures. In conductus with caudae, the mode can normally be presumed to be that which

is set by the ligature patterns seen in them, although one will always find places where it is difficult to determine exactly how the pattern is to be applied. For conductus without caudae, the only possible guide, not always a safe one, is the metric pattern of the text. This difficulty of indicating accurately the proper rhythmic mode was to lead to further notational developments to take care of the problem. We will discuss this further in speaking of the motet, like the conductus a category based on syllabic settings.

As an example of how the problem may be solved, as well as a sample of the style, we insert here the beginning of one strophe of the conductus, "Gaude virgo virginum," in honor of the Blessed Virgin Mary (Example 6-10). The opening section is the cauda, evidently in the first rhythmic mode; this mode is then applied to the beginning of the strophe, at the point where the word "In" has been inserted in brackets.

**EXAMPLE 6-10.**

While the greater part of the sources of early Notre Dame are devoted to the categories mentioned (organum for Vespers and Matins, the Gradual and the Alleluia of the Proper of the Mass, and conductus), certain other forms are also represented, forms already noted as important accretions to the liturgy. Among these other items, there are polyphonic Sequences, troped parts of the Ordinary (the Kyrie, Sanctus, and Agnus Dei), and a handful of Offertories. All these emphasize the expansion of polyphony into those areas originally explored by musicians working with monophony. They indicate the concept that no part of the liturgy was considered as incapable of polyphonic elaboration, except those chants reserved for performance by the choir. By the end of the thirteenth century, even this restriction no longer applied and composers felt free to use polyphony at their own discretion, without reference to liturgical custom.

## THE MOTET

In speaking of the work of Perotin and his immediate successors, we have noted a concentration of compositional energies upon the substitute clausula, that small form designed to abbreviate organum by the replacement of organum-style sections by new ones in discantus. By their character as separate sections, these clausulae have completeness as musical entities, without close relation to their liturgical position except in the tenor's use of a liturgically determined bit of plainchant. From their plentifulness in the sources, we may assume that such clausulae must have often been performed separately and at times not necessarily in keeping with their functional role as a portion of liturgically oriented organum; if an abbreviating substitute had been all that was required, there would have been no real reason to compose more than one clausula for each piece of organum needing shortening. A substitute, if written solely for liturgical purposes, would have been capable of but one performance each year.

Without a text, except that in the liturgical tenor, there could be little meaning in separate performance. To solve this problem, to give the substitute clausula validity as an isolated work, composers of Perotin's time, at the beginning of the thirteenth century, turned to a technique already used in a similar situation in the past, the technique of the trope. Just as words had been added to a preexisting melody to produce the trope and sequence, so now words were added to the composed polyphonic voices of the substitute clausula to produce the thirteenth-century *motet;* the name is derived from the French "mot" or "word." As polyphony had begun as a musical troping of a chant, so the motet in its beginnings developed as a poetic trope added to a musical trope; the medieval reverence for reliance on authority is obvious.

In the earliest motets, the music of the clausula remained the same, while the upper voice or voices received a Latin text that was a paraphrase or glossing of the meaning of the text carried by the plainchant tenor, this last now performed instrumentally. A second stage saw the rise of double and triple motets, termed thus according to the number of differing texts in the upper two or three voices; these too were in Latin and explained the meaning of the tenor's text. In a third stage, the language shifted to French and lost its paraphrase quality, ridding itself of any reference to the tenor. In all of these earliest motets, the music of the original clausula acted as the basic structure for poetic elaboration, just as the *jubilus* had served the first sequences.

The final development within the motet of Perotin's time was the taking over of a clausula for two voices, the troping of the duplum (now called the *motetus*) and the adding of a newly composed third voice in the same musical style. These French double motets mark the change from an originally secondary place as troped clausulae to a new position as independent forms, to be developed without reference to the liturgical background from which they came. With the possibilities opened by the entry of free composition into the motet, the interest in organa and conductus, so strong in the late twelfth century, declined rapidly; after Perotin no new works were added to the repertoire of these forms, the old ones sufficing for all liturgical needs. Indeed, it was not long until the motet was recognized as a superior category, of particular interest for the educated; although it grew, like conductus, out of clerical circles, it soon became the major musical delight of courtly society.

With the establishment of the motet as a distinct category, composers moved on to the problem of giving it a stylistic basis that would rid it of its ties to the clausula. To the middle of the thirteenth century, the composed French and Latin double motets carried most of the innovations, with the major effort given toward individualization of the three voices, one from the other. The solution finally achieved was based on rhythmic differentiation, the tenor having a slow movement, the motetus a faster one, and the triplum the fastest. The rhythmic modes were not discarded, however, for all three voices remained subject to them. The technique can be seen in Example 6-11, the opening of the Latin double motet, "O Maria virgo—O Maria maris stella—In veritate," based on the version found in the La Clayette manuscript; this source contains a repertoire dating from the second quarter of the century.

The voices here clearly contrast with each other, the tenor being in fifth mode, the motetus in first, and the triplum in sixth. The example also indicates a change in performance practice, namely that the speed of a piece was no longer dependent upon the longa as the metric unit but was turning to the brevis as the note value determining the pulse. Our transcription has, therefore, been written with a longa of three breves notated as a dotted half, not the dotted quarter of our earlier examples. Further, another value has been added, the semibrevis, equalling one-half or one-third of the brevis (measure 9 of the triplum), here shown as an eighth.

**EXAMPLE 6-11.**

In speaking of conductus, we noted the difficulties encountered in understanding which rhythmic mode to apply in works without caudae. Like conductus, the motetus and triplum of the motet gave no chance for the performer to recognize the proper mode easily, for there were almost no ligatures left in these voices; in Example 6-11, there are but four in the triplum and but six in the motetus of the entire piece, none of them of great use in defining the rhythmic mode. Only the tenor, because of its melismatic character, could preserve a ligature pattern, and it, because of its slower nature, was usually confined to the fifth mode; a ligature pattern was used for convenience in writing, not always for definition of the mode. As long as the motet had been but a troped clausula, reference to the original, or recalling its character, would give clues. With newly composed works, this procedure was manifestly impossible; the correct mode would have to be inferred from the music as it was notated.

The problem of rhythm became even more pressing because, to conserve space, the writing of a composition in score format was soon dropped. If written in score, it was possible to assure agreement of the voices, even if the mode were misinterpreted. But, in this procedure, there would of necessity be much wasted space, for all voices would have to be aligned upon the triplum, the voice with the greatest number of notes; most tripla contain at least three to four times as many as in the tenor, and they have a text that requires extra room. The method finally worked out involved the copying of each voice in succession, in what is known as choirbook format; in this, the triplum is copied above at the left, the motetus above at the right, and the tenor below, under both upper voices. To suggest the saving of space by this new method, in the La Clayette manuscript the complete motet of Example 6-11 takes ten lines for the triplum, eight for the motetus, and only two for the tenor. Only twenty lines are needed, while at least thirty would have been required to copy the work in score.

The answer to the problems of rhythm and co-ordination of voices was found by developing a new approach to rhythmic notation, taking into account the new demands for specification of individual note-values, not based upon their place within a ligated group. This new notation, called mensural notation, retained many of the external features of modal notation but defined the relation of individual notes to each other more or less clearly. With *simplices,* there was an adoption of a specific note form for the particular value desired, so that the longa, brevis, and semibrevis could be distinguished clearly as individual values. The ligature shapes of modal notation were not discarded, however, and, in melismatic passages, were still used with much the same purpose as the modern slur. Within the ligature, in spite of a superficial resemblance to past practice, the same kind of definition was made, altering the shapes slightly to indicate a specific mensural value for the individual notes within the ligature, not as a modal grouping. The lengths of rests were also defined, their values determined by the number of spaces on the staff they covered.

By around 1260, the shift to mensural notation was almost complete, in a form known as Franconian notation. Its name is derived from that of the theorist, Franco of Cologne, whose treatise, the *Ars cantus mensurabilis,* is our major source of information. The advances of pre-

Franconian notation, while great, had still many areas of ambiguity left from the vestiges of modal notation; Franco's treatise shows the final victory of the notational needs of the motet. Although traces of modal notation can still be found into the early fourteenth century, the system as described by Franco went far to solve the problems caused by the inability of modal notation and its emphasis on groups of notes to cope with the needs of the motet and its stress on the individual note.

So far as musical style is concerned, the major developments of the latter half of the thirteenth century consisted of explorations of the new paths opened by composers of the first half. Within the triplum, the process of greater differentiation continued, with the use of the semibrevis now becoming almost constant, rather than an extraordinary insertion. A feature of the motet of the third quarter of the century is the presence of many consecutive groups of semibreves, separated from each other by the device of the point. While at the beginning these groups had been restricted to no more than three semibreves, by the end of the century theorists had begun to talk of the possibility of using anywhere from two to nine semibreves as equivalent in value to one brevis; Pierre de la Croix is mentioned by these writers as the composer responsible, although only two works can be securely attributed to him. Several compositions are preserved, however, that show this increased activity within the triplum; we give the opening of one of them, "Aucun vont sovent—Amor qui cor vulnerat—Kyrieleyson" (Example 6-12), as found in a manuscript now in Turin.

**EXAMPLE 6-12.**

In the example, it will be noted that, in spite of the vast change that has come over the triplum, the motetus and tenor are still subject to modal rhythm (fifth in the tenor, second in the motetus). However, all the drive originally possessed by the rhythmic modes as used by Leonin and Perotin has disappeared. Because of the intricacy of the triplum, the motet must take its speed from that voice. Thereby the rhythmic vitality of the lower voices is destroyed, for the speed is too slow to preserve it. The most striking musical effect of this reorientation and shift of importance from the tenor to the triplum is the change in character of many tenors. Many now have no longer any pretense of a pattern of their own; instead, they consist of nothing but a series of longae, all of equal value. The tenor of our example is one of these, for it is a series of twenty longae closed by a brevis rest, with a subsequent repetition of the original series. When there is a tenor pattern, it is not as obvious as those of earlier motets, for it is now longer and has much more variety in note values. Because of the slow pace at which it must be sung and the varied shape of the pattern, the ear is much less aware of the arrangement than with previous tenors.

In the beginning, because of its liturgical origins and its semiliturgical position, the motet had by definition been based upon a plainchant tenor. By the closing years of the century, this restriction no longer applied and tenors are found to be taken from all kinds of sources. Some works do use a liturgically derived tenor but fail to identify it, giving instead the simple "Tenor" or "Neumes." Others draw directly upon secular melodies, using them as sources of a *cantus prius factus* as though they were plainchant. Some cite the borrowed secular work completely in its original form; these motets, known as French triple motets, are unusual in that all voices, including the tenor, are sung to full texts and in that the motetus and triplum reflect the rhythmic organization of the tenor rather than differentiating themselves from it. Others go to the extreme length of using a freely composed tenor as in conductus. In many cases, even when the tenor is derived from plainchant, it may be formally organized into a secular form, complete with refrains.

The tenor is not the only voice to be subjected to secular infiltration, for the other voices show the same kind of intrusions. Pre-existent secular melodies are quoted in many motets with their original texts, either in fragments or complete. The texts themselves become more secular, far more so than those of the earlier French double motets. The later motet sees the appearance of all types of non-liturgical texts, to the point of including many censuring the priesthood and condemning vices then current among clerics; one important source of the late motet, the Fauvel manuscript (Paris, Bib. Nat., fr. 146) dating from 1316, uses this type of motet as its basic constituent. Finally, whereas the French texts of earlier motets had often been translations of Latin ones, the reverse is now more frequently true.

Bamberg, Staatsbibliothek, Ed. N. 6, folio 11 recto. The motet given here shows clearly the typical arrangement of voices, the triplum at the upper left, the motetus at the upper right, and the tenor across the bottom of the page.

This invasion of the motet by outside musical influences indicates something of its high position, for, as the center of the repertoire, it acted as a magnet for all kinds of musical expression. Just as it attracted to itself from all sides and from all categories, so also did it furnish something of itself to forms no longer favored. We have noted the disappearance of newly composed conductus and organa; the motet made up for the loss. It one drops the tenor of a motet and if the two upper voices are either retained or are given the same text, one has something like conductus; if one removes the text of a motet, one has something like a substitute clausula. Both procedures were followed in the late thirteenth century.

Our sources for the Notre Dame motet are the same four manuscripts mentioned earlier, plus two important sources that are completely devoted to the motet. The largest of the latter is the Montpellier manuscript, H 196, referred to as Mo; the other great motet source is Bamberg, Ed. N. 6, abbreviated Ba. These two sources include motets of the early period as well as the later. In addition, there are many other sources, peripheral in nature, that indicate the wide spread of Notre Dame techniques. These come from many parts of Europe, England, Germany, Flanders, and Spain, as well as outlying parts of France itself, and all show an awareness of Parisian accomplishments, but with local characteristics well to the fore. Not only do these manuscripts include many works of French origin, but they also provide evidence that certain categories, notably the polyphonic trope and sequence, were still popular in these areas, although no longer extensively cultivated by Notre Dame. To these types of works was applied the new motet technique, leading to a paraphrase procedure that persisted in certain areas, England and Avignon in particular, until well into the fourteenth century.

## SECULAR POLYPHONY

At the beginning of the thirteenth century, there were in France two distinct categories, sacred polyphony and secular monophony, clearly different in function, audience, and technique. By the end of the century, the once carefully drawn lines between the two had blurred to the point that, in speaking of the motet, it would be impossible to label it as completely one or the other; the techniques are generally those of sacred polyphony, while the larger part of the textual and melodic elements are those of secular monophony. What had begun originally as a musical manifestation of a clerical group had become the social amusement of a nobility which had discarded what had been its own, the monophonic trouvère art.

The reasons for the many changes found in the motet after the middle of the century, especially the intrusion of secular elements, seem to lie in the increasing secularization within the clergy and in the desire of the noble laity to adopt for their own purposes the evident superiority of polyphony. That clerical society was no longer unaware of the beauties of the outside world is evident in the texts of many motets composed after the second quarter of the century; echoes of the Goliardic spirit are common, and the many reproaches leveled against priests of all ranks who had forgotten their vows, found in motets from Ba to Fauvel, show an awareness of the loss of spirituality. The Albigensian and Waldensian heresies and the difficulties involved in stamping them out are further evidence of a rise of anti-clericalism, a falling away from respect for the Church and its servants that even the establishment of the Franciscan and Dominican orders of mendicant monks, with their new appeal, could do little to check. The demarcation between cleric and laity in terms of liking for the good things of life was no longer distinct.

With this lack of cleavage in social outlook, the personal goals of both classes were quite close. When the nobility had recognized the higher interest of polyphony and desired it for their own, there was little difficulty in getting those most skilled in its production to turn their talents in a secular direction. In the same spirit with which earlier composers had provided polyphonic works for the embellishment of the liturgy, later composers wrote polyphony for the enhancement of courtly occasions. Originally provided for only the highest festivities such as coronations or other situations of a somewhat liturgical character, but soon spreading to all kinds of secular occasions, the new polyphony rapidly adopted those characteristics that would please its new audience. The effort to delight the now primarily laic listeners required the use of texts, forms, and melodies already familiar, or their derivations; the audience was no longer limited to the Church but was now that which had formerly cultivated the trouvère. This noble public was not one trained in the scholastic tradition, with its emphasis on the speculative, but was the cultured upper class, appreciative of the beauties of well-organized sound and understanding music more as an *ars* than a *scientia*.

Since the composer of motets for this group was normally a cleric, his approach to secular polyphony was primarily through the motet and the techniques developed therein, fitting the new secular material to its context. During the thirteenth century little effort was made to apply polyphony to those forms developed by secular musicians, namely the rondeau, virelai, and ballade. In France, the only figure who seems to have undertaken polyphonic settings of these forms is Adam de la Halle (1240?–1288?), a bourgeois musician from Arras, whose *Robin et Marion* is a play with interspersed monophonic melodies. Adam has left seven motets and sixteen polyphonic *rondels,* of which fourteen are rondeaux, one a virelai, and another a ballade. All sixteen of these last are in conductus style, an approach long discarded for the upper-level art work, but probably adopted here by the nature of the audience. The music to "Je muir d'amourete" ("I die of love") will show the manner (Example 6-13).

EXAMPLE 6-13.

Je muir, je muir    d'a - mou - ret - te,    las ai - mi,

Par de - fau - te    d'a - mi - e - te    de mer - chi.

The most famous piece of secular polyphony is the Reading Rota, "Sumer is icumen in," from the third quarter of the century. This work is for six voices, four in canon on the principal melody, two others in canon on a short fragment that acts as a foundation (the *pes*). In canonic technique, it is one of the more ambitious works of its time; the continent saw nothing like this. As with many motets of the same time, the Rota carries the possibility of performance in Latin; a second text, "Perspice Christicola," has been inserted below the English one. The British Museum manuscript including this work also contains three polyphonic dances, indicating the beginning of the spread of the new technique into this genre. Although there are many indications that polyphony had already begun to play a large role in dance music, most of it seems to have been improvised and thus has not come down to us.

The early thirteenth century marks the high point of medieval music, for it is during this period that the highest degree of union existed between aesthetic goal and artistic fulfillment of that goal. Until that time, the history of music had seen the steady expansion of technique and artistic achievement toward the creation of a repertoire that would satisfy both the demand of the creators themselves for musical interest and that of theologians who had defined the purposes for which music was to be used. There had been no conflict of interest during the preceding centuries, for it was a true partnership, the *cantor* working always in complete harmony with the *musicus*. The functional and philosophical aspects of music worked together, the performer thoroughly understanding his place within the philosophical framework, the speculator comprehending the technical interests of the practitioner.

The creations of this Golden Age reflect this unity, for the work of Leonin and Perotin clearly shows the urge to serve the aesthetic goal set forth by the Church and its thinkers. The technical miracles produced by these men and their contemporaries were reflections in sound of the philosophical developments brought to a peak at about the same time by St. Bonaventura and St. Thomas Aquinas. Just as these men were trying to explore the nature of God and his creations by reason, so were musicians attempting to mirror the glory of these creations and the reasonableness of their multiform manifestations in sound. As Notre Dame was a replica of the orderliness of God's world in stone, so were the works of its musicians a reflection of that universe in music.

With the advancing thirteenth century, the paths of philosopher and musician began to diverge. Where adjustments of the one to the needs of the other had previously been made without effort and with alacrity, there were now increasing indications of a basic split in the understanding of a common goal, combined with further evidence that this goal no longer carried meaning. In philosophy, after St. Thomas there was more and more a tendency to degrade what had been, in his hands, a fruitful inquiry to a repetitious mouthing of formulae and intricacies without life or validity; with Duns Scotus (1270?–1308) and William of Occam (1300?–1349), medieval philosophy had lost its drive. In music, the liturgy and its embellishment no longer had overpowering interest for the composer. His concern with the development of technique was now increasingly for its own sake; all was done without great regard for the purposes to which technique might be put or the fitness of the results to that spiritual goal which had originally been behind his creations.

No better evidence of this failure on the musician's part is to be found than the growing number of complaints heard from the Church on the abuses of music and its disregard for liturgical function. Roger Bacon, for one, observed the continual quest in Paris for novelty, leading to excesses that perverted liturgical sanctity. Condemnation of the use of French motet texts as performed in monasteries became constant after the middle of the century, with a particularly strong blast appearing in 1275 against motet-singing in churches. Already, around 1250, the Cistercians and Dominicans had formally forbidden polyphony as a "disturbance" to the service. Nowhere does the emphasis on technique without higher goal appear more clearly than in the violent diatribes—against the excessive liberties taken by the "moderns"—written by Jacques de Liège, whose *Speculum musicae* comes from the beginning of the fourteenth century; to Jacques, all sense of continuity had been lost and no understanding of music's higher goals remained. With the bull of Pope John XXII from around 1324, the situation was clearly recognized. While organum in the older manner was approved as an aid to devotion, all the latter innovations and elaborations were condemned in their entirety, anathematized as completely outside the spiritual purposes of music. Specifically forbidden were rhythmic deformations of plainchant, the use of the vernacular, the appearance of *hoquet* (a breaking up of a line between two voices by singing its individual notes in rapid alternation), and the employment of rapid chains of notes in small values.

But the temper of the changing times was such that all these complaints had little or no effect. Composers kept on exploring musical possibilities without regard for criticism and, what is more to the point, continued to compose religious music in the new manner, the resulting works then being performed as part of the liturgy. Following generations were well aware of the philosophical implications that music was thought to contain, but their awareness was more lip service than obedience; secularization and, with it, the birth pangs of the Renaissance to come had concentrated their attention on music's more sensual elements. *Musica instrumentalis* was on its way to becoming the master and the focus of interest.

## BIBLIOGRAPHICAL NOTES

For the innovations of Notre Dame, the outstanding source is still William G. Waite, *The Rhythm of Twelfth Century Polyphony* (New Haven: Yale University Press, 1954); the latter part of the volume includes a complete transcription of the *Magnus Liber*. For the notation, Willi Apel's *The Notation of Polyphonic Music* (Cambridge: Mediaeval Academy, many eds.) is the standard reference work. The major sources of the period have been published in facsimile; W[1] is given in J. H. Baxter, *An Old St. Andrews Music Book* (London: Humphrey Milford, 1931), W[2], F, Ma, and many others published over the last fifteen years by the Institute of Mediaeval Music, Brooklyn. Mo is given in facsimile and transcription in Yvonne Rokseth's *Polyphonies du XIIIe Siècle* (Paris: Oiseau-Lyre, 4 vols., 1939); Ba has been similarly edited by Pierre

Aubry, *Cent motets du XIIIe siècle* (Paris: Rouart, 3 vols., 1908). Paris, Bibliothèque Nationale, lat. 15139 (the St. Victor manuscript), has been edited in facsimile by Ethel Thurston (Toronto: Pontifical Institute of Mediaeval Studies, 1959); she has also edited *The Works of Perotin* (New York: E. F. Kalmus, 1970).

Published transcriptions of the music of Notre Dame are too numerous to list here in detail. The transcriptions of Mo by Rokseth and Ba by Aubry have been mentioned above. Hans Tischler has announced the publication of the entire corpus of motets, although no publication date has been set. Janet Knapp's *Thirty-Five Conductus* (*Yale Collegium Musicum*, 6) (New Haven: Yale University, 1965) is an excellent small collection of this category. Nigel E. Wilkins has transcribed the works of Adam de la Halle for the American Institute of Musicology (*CMM* 44).

There are many articles on special topics of concern in such journals as *Speculum, Acta Musicologica, Journal of the American Musicological Society, Musica Disciplina,* and *Musical Quarterly;* the authorities in English are, in addition to Waite and Tischler, Luther Dittmer, Willi Apel, Gordon A. Anderson, Janet Knapp, and Frank Ll. Harrison. For the reader of French, the study of the motet as given by Yvonne Rokseth in *Polyphonies* . . . is classic; all present-day studies begin here. Two articles that deserve special mention are Norman E. Smith, "Tenor Repetition in the Notre Dame Organa," *Journal of the American Musicological Society,* XIX (1966), and Gordon A. Anderson, "Notre Dame Latin Double Motets," *Musica Disciplina,* XXV (1971). The fundamental work in German is Friedrich Ludwig, *Repertorium organorum* (Halle: Niemayer, 1910); incomplete, it is being revised and completed by Luther Dittmer for the Institute of Mediaeval Music.

# SEVEN

# THE FRENCH ARS NOVA

With the fourteenth century, the dissolution of the medieval world, already intimated in the closing years of the preceding century, becomes obvious. The Great Jubilee of 1300, that great Roman pageant designed by Boniface VIII to show papal supremacy, was followed almost immediately by complete ruin of all that the papacy had stood for in the nature of a supra-national state. By 1305, the papacy had embarked upon a time of troubles, starting with the Babylonian Captivity (1305–1378), when the center of the Church was outside Rome in Avignon, and only ending with the close of the Great Schism (1378–1417), during which the Christian world saw the spectacle of two rival popes and, for a time, three. To the rulers of Europe, the Pope no longer represented a spiritual head, above party strife; he had become a tool of national policies, to be controlled and directed in accord with political ambitions. During the Great Schism, allegiance to one or another pope was made only in part on spiritual bases; practical considerations often determined the choice. England chose an anti-French pope, Scotland an anti-English one; in Italy, rulers and subjects of the same area often picked opposing popes, as in Naples and Sicily.

Together with this state of anarchy within the Church went a correspondingly chaotic scene in secular affairs. Nationalistic aspirations and desire for expansion soon brought France and England into direct confrontation, with the Hundred Years' War (1338–1453) as an outgrowth of political ambitions on both sides. In Italy, small city-states continued to intrigue against each other and to engage in small wars with their neighbors; within the cities themselves, civil strife was normal, for the Guelph and Ghibelline factions were omnipresent. The Guelphs as partisans of papal and popular elements represented the efforts of the middle classes to move against the Ghibellines, the supporters of the Holy Roman Emperor and the nobility. In Spain, although successful in clearing the Moors from the peninsula, the various kingdoms found themselves continually embroiled in dynastic problems and in an inability to control the increasingly insurgent nobility; internal difficulties were compounded by the need to steer a careful course between the two giants, France and England. In Germany, the battle of the towns against the princes was a major preoccupation; for a time, the Hanseatic League threatened to become a major power. German unification made a few feeble beginnings, but, faced with simultaneous problems on all borders, and with internal dissensions, it made no progress; the low state of German affairs may be seen in the simultaneous appearance of three rival Holy Roman Emperors (1400–1410), a situation like that of the papacy at the same time.

To complicate all these problems, in the middle of the century Europe was swept by the Black Death, which reduced the population by one-third to one-half. All parts of Europe felt the impact of this loss of life, for the end result was a reduction in the labor force to such a point that, feeling his new importance, the peasant became dissatisfied with his lot. In nearly all parts of Europe, there were revolts of the lower classes in attempts to upset the established social order. None was successful, but they served to disturb the demarcation lines that had been taken for granted, stratifications that had been so characteristic of the high Middle Ages; the serf, the villein, and the peasant were to change their social conditions, just as were their betters.

The same air of disintegration is found in the music of the fourteenth century. Like the world of which it was a part, nationalism, emphasizing individual characteristics of one locality and a distinction in technical approaches from one area to another, played a major role in the musical developments of the century. Musicians were no longer recruited primarily from within the Church and, even when serving the Church, took little account of the functions their music was to serve. The interest already found in music as a technical toy became, in France by the end of the century, the overriding concern; we can only react, in all too many cases, with a certain amazement at the amount of sterile complexity and meaningless intricacy in such music.

This period is generally given the name "Ars Nova" ("New Art") by music historians. The term is derived from the title of a treatise by Philippe de Vitry (1291–1361), the theorist whose work in music as both composer and author reflects the deep nature of the changes. That the period is literally one of a "New Art" in France is obvious, for the strictures of Jacques de Liège make it evident that there were clear lines of cleavage between the novelties of the fourteenth century and thirteenth-century practices; the late thirteenth century has, for this reason, often been labled as the "Ars Antiqua," "Ars vetus," or "Old Art" by many scholars, although so described by only a handful of writers of the time.

In applying the term to developments in other countries—Italy or England, for example—there is more of a problem, for to have something new there must be something old. In the case of England, the difficulty is not serious, for English musicians had been generally oriented toward the practices of their French contemporaries from the beginning and, from the thirteenth century on, remained generally close to their principles. In Italy, as we shall see in the following chapter, there was, so far as we now know, no polyphonic art of importance before 1300, except a simple im-provisational technique whose roots lay in the work of Guido. The achievements of the fourteenth century are new only in the sense that nothing like them seems to have existed previously. Even so, the term "Ars Nova" is appropriate, for Italian music, like that of France and England, reflects the novelties of the times, the newness of an art that had to fit itself into a new place in a new society and with new functions.

The changed attitudes toward music and its place are perhaps best revealed in a survey of the theoretical sources of the period, as they reveal their purpose and their intended audience. We may begin by recalling that the general division of treatises before the rise of polyphony had been into the speculative and the practical, with the speculative designed primarily for use within the *quadrivium* and the practical intended for the singer within the Church. With the introduction of polyphony and, later, the complications of modal and mensural notation, the scope of the practical treatise had been enlarged to include the newer developments, but without losing sight of the place of these developments within the speculative framework. The compendium of Jerome of Moravia illustrates this clearly, in its inclusion of speculative elements together with practical descrip-tions of technical necessities; the philosophic viewpoints expressed in it are contemporary with those of music's practical directions. The treatise of Johannes de Grocheo from around 1300 begins with certain philosophical

foundations before proceeding to an exposition of forms and other practicalities; the two divisions are in balance.

With the fourteenth century, the decline of the purely speculative
treatise becomes evident. In France, the final great example comes from
shortly after 1300, the *Speculum Musicae* of Jacques de Liège. Organized
in seven books, the work is obviously intended for the embryo philosopher; the first five books generally follow the guidance and example of
Boethius and only the last two can be considered as treating practical
matters. There is, throughout the work, an air of frustration, an under-
current of anger that implies a realization on Jacques's part that his labor
has been passed by and that his work is already doomed to oblivion. In
Italy, the last large speculatively oriented work is that of Ugolino of
Orvieto, the *Declaratio Musicae Disciplinae,* a treatise which, like that of
Jacques, bases much of its organization and discussion on Boethius; it too
is out of touch with its own time in some ways, for its third book is an extended gloss on a treatise of Johannes de Muris (1290?–1351?), which was
then almost a century old.

The decline in interest in the speculative as part of the practically
directed treatise may in part be traced to an overpowering fascination
with technical novelties and a lessened dependence of such innovations
upon philosophical justification. Indeed, many works suggest an impa-
tience with the older need to begin with a speculative foundation. Several
treatises of the fourteenth century have as their opening phrase, "Gaudent
brevitate moderni" ("Modern men rejoice in brevity"), and then proceed
without further ado to the practicalities that are the purpose of the exposition. The new audience implied is one whose intentions are not those of
the university student or the performing churchman; it is one that is beginning to regard music as a fine art, not a liberal art.

Within the purely practical treatise, the emphasis falls primarily
upon the new mensural and notational innovations. Although treatises
sometimes include material on plainchant, the modes, and their performance, together with directions for the improvising of simple note-
against-note polyphony, the normal tendency in most sources is to provide
nothing new here; many manuscripts merely include copies of older
treatises discussing these subjects, with the newer treatises beginning at
once with the novelties in polyphonic composition. Few works discuss
both monophony and polyphony as part of a larger plan; the older
treatises have discussed monophony well enough, so the modern ones
omit its description, in favor of matters of more importance to their
authors.

In France, the novelties of so much interest to the fourteenth century were centered about new ways of mensuration, and the development
of means of notating them clearly. In addition, certain approaches to

musical complication already inherent in the late thirteenth century led to characteristic forms, such as the isorhythmic motet and a new emphasis on the Ordinary of the Mass, and to the expansion of polyphony to areas hardly touched earlier, the secular forms such as the ballade, rondeau, and virelai. Similar processes were at work in Italy, to be discussed in our following chapter. At the beginning, the results within the two countries were different, but, by the end of the century, French procedures had proven their superiority, with a consequent disappearance of purely Italian methods.

## NOVELTIES OF THE ARS NOVA: MENSURATION

To the end of the thirteenth century and the work of Pierre de la Croix, the essential rhythmic patterns had been those based on triple groupings, the longa being divided into three breves. All six rhythmic modes reflect this situation, for, even when two breves are to be considered equivalent in time value to a longa, the second brevis is altered, that is, made double its normal length, so that it, with its companion, will complete a unit of three parts. From its triple nature, like that of the Trinity, this mensuration was given the designation "perfect" and was originally considered as the only possible one, the sole mensuration justifiable on speculative grounds.

Imperfect mensuration, that based on duple divisions, was, however, beginning to appear in the latter part of the thirteenth century, for both Mo and Ba contain motets written in this fashion. In these the longa is divided into two breves of equal value. But, it spite of the evident interest taken in imperfect mensuration, particularly by English composers, it did not have the same speculative and philosophical distinction; its denomination as imperfect shows its lower place. The Reading Rota, "Sumer is icumen in," was originally written in imperfect mensuration and later revised by a following scribe to perfect; this may have been done to allow performance of the Latin contrafactum in religious circumstances.

With the Fauvel manuscript of around 1316, the status of imperfect mensuration was well advanced, indicating that, regardless of its philosophical position, it was an accepted part of compositional procedures. The official recognition of the equality of perfect and imperfect mensurations comes, however, with de Vitry's Ars Nova of the third decade of the century, where his discussion makes no intimations of superiority or inferiority on the part of one or the other; henceforth, perfect and imperfect are to be considered as simple appellations indicative of triple or duple divisions within the notational unit, with no great overtones of speculative import.

At the end of the thirteenth century, only four values of notes were specified, the maxima or duplex longa, the longa, the brevis, and the semibrevis:

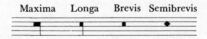

Certain difficulties had, however, become obvious, for, with the change of the temporal unit from the longa to the brevis and the slowing down of the beat, the necessity of finding a smaller value than the semibrevis was apparent. The solution of allowing the brevis to be divided into as many as nine semibreves, thus reducing their effective value in various ways, was evidently but an expedient; if a brevis were taken as the temporal unit, some way was needed to determine the interrelationship of the semibreves within the brevis.

One solution, described by the Italian theorist Marchettus of Padua in his *Pomerium* (1324–1326) and utilized in Fauvel, was the provision of a set of rhythmic formulae covering situations of from two to six semibreves in a group. The essence of the system was the assumption that the longer value or values come in the closing part of the group. This was called "the path of nature" (Example 7-1a). If, however, the longer value was to come at another point, the simple shape of the semibreve was altered by the addition of a tail, extended downward; this was called "the path of art" (Example 7-1b). For example, if, in a unit of two semibreves, the first has a tail, it is the longer note of the two; in the transcription ratio of our example, a half note precedes the quarter.

**EXAMPLE 7-1.**

With the use of the tailed note, the system became somewhat elastic. However, while useful, it was more a regression than an advance, for it was a return to much the same principles as those of modal notation.

A second solution, probably developed in the College of Navarre in Paris about the same time, was the introduction of a fifth note shape called the minima, indicating a temporal value one level below the semi-brevis; its form is that of the semibrevis with a tail extended upward: ▮. To this value were applied the same principles of relationship already outlined by Franco in the previous century for the longa-brevis relation-ship.

The mensural system as developed by de Vitry and his followers, de Muris, and others, is based on the possibility of a triple or duple rela-tionship at any of several levels. At the very top is that between maxima and longa, *maximodus,* theoretically possible although seldom seen; this is followed by *modus,* the relationship between longa and brevis; *tempus,* that between brevis and semibrevis; and *prolatio,* that between semibrevis and minima. To assist the performer in understanding which type of men-suration was to be used, de Vitry introduced the idea of the time signa-ture to show *modus* and *tempus;* the first was represented by a rectangle including two or three small dashes, the second by a circle for perfect and a half circle for imperfect. Later theorists were to revises the system slightly and add details to these last two symbols to indicate *prolatio;* a point within the circle or half circle indicated *prolatio maior,* the plain circle or half circle *prolatio minor.* If the minima be taken as an eighth note, Example 7-2 shows the modern equivalents of the various time sig-natures on the level of *tempus* and *prolatio.*

**EXAMPLE 7-2.**

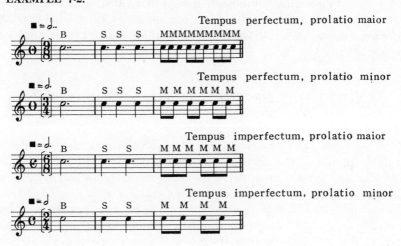

In many sources of the fourteenth century no time signatures are given, and one of the major sections of many treatises from the period is often a series of elaborate rules to help the student or performer determine the correct mensuration by inspection. One device of importance, described by de Vitry and amplified in its use by his successors, was the introduction of red notes into the music, to show shifts in mensuration or to indicate changes in value from those designated by the normal black notes; in some sources a note only outlined in black, a "white" note, served the same purpose. This innovation, giving a certain exoticism and brilliance to the manuscript sources, was developed to a high point, for, following the lead of de Vitry, various shapes of notes in both black and red were devised, all to indicate values not easily written in the normal manner.

A final novelty, similarly of great importance, was the use of the point after a given note, not only to indicate an addition of length to its normal value but also as a way of dividing groups of notes from each other, to aid in the indication of syncopation. Not discussed by de Vitry, but seen in the examples of his *Ars Nova*, the use of the point as a way of defining mensural combinations was to lead to possibilities of immense rhythmic complexity and elaborateness.

While the general principles of mensuration and notation were well established by de Vitry and his immediate followers, a tremendous range of individuality exists in the practical sources, for they show no real uniformity in their notational procedures. The general impression gained from study of the manuscripts is that practice was moving more rapidly than its codification and that the notational needs of the composer were satisfied by solutions that were individual and without relation to an already established system. The composer knew what rhythmic arrangements he wished to write and devised his answers to the problems as they occurred.

## NOVELTIES OF THE ARS NOVA: ISORHYTHM

As early as the introduction of the substitute clausula by Perotin at the beginning of the thirteenth century, it was evident that, to achieve any degree of length, repetition of the fundamental tenor had to be made. In many of these works, therefore, we note that the tenor may be repeated several times, in order to provide the composer with a sufficiently long foundation. At the century passed, this repetition became less mechanical and, in the later manuscripts, began to show a more imaginative approach, with the tenor being repeated as in a refrain form or in a manner that was to become the method followed by composers of the Ars Nova, the method of isorhythm.

To understand this isorhythmic technique, it is perhaps easiest to consider a given melody, the tenor, as the composers of the Ars Nova did —a combination of two elements, melody and rhythm. The melody, called the *color,* was taken as a series of pitches, without rhythm and without necessity for retention of a specific melodic shape. To this series of pitches, the composer then applied a specific rhythmic pattern, the *talea* ("cutting"), a rhythmic organization not necessarily related to that of the original melody. To this pattern or *talea* the original pitch sequence or *color* was fitted, so that the final product was a combination of the two elements, both being repeated. Thus far, there is little real distinction between this method and the older one of literal repetition, for one could speak of a literal repetition as one of the *color* and of the *talea,* if the rhythmic pattern of the original melody is considered as a *talea* in its entirety.

Where the novelty came in isorhythm was the desire of the composer to provide non-coincidence in length between the *color* and the *talea.* Thus if the melody included twenty notes, for example, and the rhythmic pattern decided upon used only fifteen of these, the *color* would begin its repetition after the *talea* had recommenced; there would be an overlapping of the first part of the new *talea* with the last of the *color.* If the process were continued to a point of final coincidence, it would require four repetitions of the *color* and five of the *talea.* In Example 7-3, we show the process on a small scale, with a *color* of six notes and a *talea* of five; the beginning of each *color* is marked with a Roman numeral, that of each *talea* with a letter.

**EXAMPLE 7-3.**

With this technique as a foundation, numerous variations were possible. In many isorhythmic motets, the closing portion of the work will find the tenor using the original *talea* in shortened values, giving a quickened pace that acts as a coda to the work. The length of *color* and *talea* were not prescribed, so that the *color* might be shorter than the *talea*, or vice versa. The isorhythmic process may be reflected in the upper voices, with the appearance of particular rhythmic patterns, which are repeated in the manner of a *talea;* to these, the proper term to be applied is isometric, for there is, in these voices, no effort to maintain strict adherence to a repeated pitch pattern as well.

In its fully developed form, the isorhythmic motet begins with preparation of an isorhythmic tenor, its *color* normally based on some kind of pre-existing melody, either sacred or secular or, in some cases, free-composed. Above this tenor the composer adds two or three voices, one or all of these involving the repetition of rhythmic patterns. The whole receives its name from the isorhythmic character of the tenor. Like the motet of the late thirteenth century, there is normally an attempt to differentiate voices by their speeds; the tenor, as before, is the slowest voice, with the motetus and triplum in contrasting faster rhythms.

The isorhythmic motet is the major art form of the French Ars Nova, just as organum and the motet were those of the Ars Antiqua. Its rhythmical severity and intensely patterned course were obvious sources of delight to the cultured listener and provided for him the same intellectual pleasure that later generations were to derive from the fugue and the symphony. There is, within the isorhythmic motet, much the same approach to intellectuality as today in serial composition, with its strict arrangement of patterns of all types; twelve-tone composition is, in many ways, a modern application of the principle of *color* repetition.

The major sources for the repertoire of the isorhythmic motet in the early fourteenth century are the Fauvel manuscript, already mentioned, and a codex from Ivrea. The Fauvel source is among the most interesting of all our manuscripts, for it is basically a long poem by Gervais du Bus with additions by Raoul Chaillou. Within the poem, many charges are brought against the Church, the whole taking on the form of the medieval *admonitio;* the full title of the work, *Le Roman de Fauvel*, is derived from the personalization of the stallion, Fauvel, a symbol of the vices of the Church, whose name is taken from the initial letters of the seven vices, Flattery, Avarice, Villainy, Variability, Envy, and Looseness. In addition to many monophonic works, the manuscript contains 34 poly-

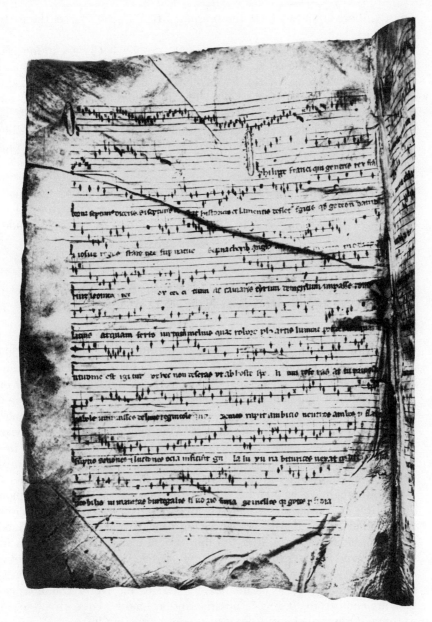

Ivrea, Biblioteca Capitolare, folio 1 verso. The music here is the triplum of the anonymous motet, "O Philippe Franci," written for Philippe VI of France (1293–1350).

phonic compositions as interpolations. Although the greater part of these musical insertions are representative of the latter part of the thirteenth century, there are a few from the presumed time of the source, the early fourteenth century.

The Ivrea codex, from around 1360, is somewhat larger in musical content, for it includes 81 compositions—motets, Mass sections, and French secular works. Of the 14 motets now accepted definitely as the work of de Vitry, it contains 9. Unlike Fauvel, it does not hark back to the previous century, but represents a repertoire from around the middle of the fourteenth century and slightly earlier. One of the most interesting features of its contents is the balance between the motet and other compositional categories; slightly less than half the compositions represented are motets, with 37 in all. There is thus some suggestion that interest in the motet had begun to fade slightly, and that, although it was to remain at the center of the repertoire into the fifteenth century, other forms had become of sufficient interest to attract the attention of more and more composers.

## NOVELTIES OF THE ARS NOVA:
## MASS MOVEMENTS AND MASSES

With the transfer of the papacy from Rome to Avignon in 1305 and the rapid growth of court life there, a rival to Paris as a cultural center was quickly established. Under John XXII (1313–1334), the author of the famous bull mentioned at the close of the preceding chapter, new methods of raising funds for the religious hierarchy in its new French home had been found, bringing in more than enough to finance a lavish scale of living. As a part of the papal household, musicians held an important position, not only as members of a liturgical choir but also as providers of entertainment for the leisure hours of the Pope and his retinue.

Although we cannot be sure of the musical climate in Avignon during the first years of the Babylonian Captivity, the Ivrea manuscript and another found at Apt, both deriving from Avignon, give some idea of the shifts taking place after the third quarter of the century, both in technique and in repertoire. The essential change lies in the creation of a new category, involving the polyphonic setting of movements of the Ordinary of the Mass. While Ordinaries are part of the Notre Dame scene, they are comparatively few in number and are most frequently attached to troped Ordinary chants, the normal ones appearing infrequently. Certain items, the Gloria and Credo, are seldom set, in any manner; indeed, the Credo is, by its nature, not to be expected. The Kyrie, Sanctus, and Agnus had received the greater attention, perhaps because of their shorter texts.

In mid-century Avignon, to judge from the Ivrea manuscript, the situation was completely reversed. We have already noted the lesser place of the motet in that source, 37 works of 81; what is unusual is that, within the remaining 44 works, 25 are Mass movements—4 Kyries (2 troped), 9 Glorias (3 troped), 10 Credos, 2 Sanctus sections (1 troped), and 1 indecipherable Kyrie. The emphasis in Ivrea is upon those sections previously neglected, for the Gloria and Credo settings together make up 19 of the 25 works. No Mass Propers are included nor are there compositions for the Hours; doubtless, these were improvised as needed.

The Apt manuscript, reflecting a repertoire of some 25 years later, reinforces the impression of a trend toward settings of the Ordinary, for, of its 48 compositions, only 4 are non-liturgical motets, the remaining 44 works consisting of 10 Kyries (6 troped), 9 Glorias (1 troped), 10 Credos, 4 Sanctus (1 troped), and 1 Agnus. There are also 10 Hymns; of the 10, all for 3 voices, 9 have their liturgical melody in the triplum. As in Ivrea, the number of Glorias and Credos is quite high, although not in the same overpowering proportion. To be noted is the one Agnus, a section not represented in Ivrea, as well as material for the Hours.

Having no models for a formal approach, the composers around Avignon turned to various types of compositions for their inspiration. As a primary source because of its artistic position, the motet logically furnished the first basis for the new Ordinaries; but, because of the liturgical character of the Mass, it could not be and was not taken over without change. The earliest Ordinary settings are built, like a motet, upon a tenor, but it is in most cases a non-liturgical one and does not have the same structural function as that of a motet. Instead, it acts as a harmonic support for the upper two voices, these in turn moving together on the same text in the manner of a vocal duet. The tenor may be arranged in something resembling an isorhythmic pattern, but it lacks the dependence on *color* and *talea* non-coincidence found in true isorhythm. Most of the Mass sections in Ivrea are of this type.

A second solution was found in what has been labelled discantus technique, taken from secular models without complications. Here, there is normally but one voice, the highest, which carries the liturgical text, the lower voices acting as instrumental supports. In many cases, the tenor is no longer the lowest voice, that position being taken by what is called a contratenor; both of these work together, often crossing and closely resembling each other. Evidently, the tenor has not acted as a generator for the web of the composition, but has been conceived as one of two supports for the uppermost voice; the technique is that of an accompanied vocal solo. The Apt manuscript shows a turn toward this approach, for in it the number of Mass sections in discantus is greater than that in motet style.

A final solution was conductus-like, where all voices carry the text and move together in the older manner. Whether there was actually a connection or not between the two is difficult to say, for it is possible that this particular manner was derived from the improvisatory practices so common during the period. Both Ivrea and Apt contain many examples of this procedure, suggesting that it was a well established method and one of equal interest with motet and discantus styles.

In addition to providing the first great concentration upon items of the Ordinary as individual sections to be set in polyphony, the Ars Nova also presents the first efforts to collect the various parts of the Ordinary into one unit, that is, to make of the parts a unified whole, if not by musical inter-relationships, at least by grouping the sections together as a set. The most important of the complete settings is that by Guillaume de Machaut, coming from outside the tradition of Avignon and to be discussed presently. Others exist, obviously not composed entirely by one man, yet collected together in such a way as to suggest a feeling of liturgical unity. The earliest of these is found in a manuscript from Tournai, with others appearing in sources from Toulouse, Barcelona, and the Sorbonne. In none of these is there evidence of an intent to compose the complete cycle as a unit, but rather an effort to combine individual movements into a set of Ordinaries that will function together liturgically. It is probable that the various parts of the Sorbonne Mass were the product of one man, Johannes Lambuleti (fl. 1350), but this is not yet securely proven.

Not all the cycles are complete, for the Credo is not always included. Where it is found, as in the Tournai or Toulouse Masses, it appears also as an individual movement in other sources; the Credo of both these Masses is found in Apt, that of the Toulouse Mass in Ivrea. Other movements also may not appear, as again in the Toulouse Mass, where there is no Gloria.

Recent research has indicated that there are many cross-relations between the various settings of the Ordinary made around Avignon; composers were evidently well aware of what their fellows had done. Not only is there provision of contrafacta, as in the Sorbonne Mass, where the opening Kyrie furnishes the material for the Agnus, but there is also a procedure in which sections of one composition are taken over, rearranged, and given a new text. The most complex technique is that of parody, where the polyphonic web of one piece is used as the starting point for another; this occurs in the Sorbonne Mass's first Agnus, which has its roots in an Ivrea Sanctus, this in turn being based on an Agnus coming from a third source, a manuscript now in Cambrai. As in the thirteenth century, there is ample evidence here of the continuing tradition of reference to authority and the glossing of a given text, although the reasons for the reappearance of older material seem to be based more on purely musical considerations than on philosophical ones.

## NOVELTIES OF THE ARS NOVA: SECULAR FORMS

By the end of the thirteenth century, the interest of composers had begun to turn to secular forms, although much of their use of these forms lay within the context of the motet; the repetition pattern of certain tenors within these pieces is often governed by the refrain principles of a secular form, and the musical ideas found in secular works are carried over into the more artistic form and made a part of the motet structure. Little attention, however, had been paid to the application of polyphony to the secular forms *per se,* with perhaps the only extensive effort being that of Adam de la Halle in his rondeaux.

Much the same situation can still be found in Fauvel. In spite of the large number of secular monophonic works in all the usual forms, the polyphonic compositions include few secular forms as such. Many of the motets carry secular tenors, and two of them—the Latin double motet, "Quomodo cantabimus—Thalamus puerpere," and the French double motet, "Se me desires—Bonne est amours"—in spite of their motet technique, repeat the tenor in the manner of a virelai; the relation to the secular is close. Nearer the secular are two works, "Quare fremuerunt" and "Bon vin doit," in which the first, in two voices, uses musical material taken from an earlier conductus but handling it in the manner of a motet, with the form of a ballade imposed upon the whole. The second work is a drinking song, with a short tenor phrase repeated four times; above it, the duplum and triplum carry their own texts and new music for each tenor repetition. The tenor here acts much like the "pes" of the Reading Rota, a foundation for the other parts.

Ivrea reflects the changing attitudes toward secular forms, for, among the motets and sacred compositions, one finds five rondeaux for three voices and another for four, two virelais for two voices, a double virelai, and two more for three voices. One of these last, "Or sus, vous dormez trop," is of particular interest, for it appears in four other sources, some even coming from the fifteenth century; as a song introducing imitations of bird calls, it is a forerunner of the program chanson to be developed in the sixteenth century. (And, curiously, a work by Janequin that similarly uses bird-song imitations begins with exactly the same text.) The section introducing these calls is given as Example 7-4.

**EXAMPLE 7-4.**

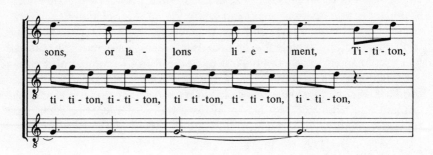

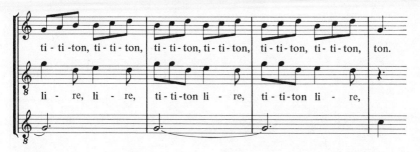

ti - ti -ton, ti - ti - ton,  ti - ti - ton, ti - ti - ton,  ti - ti - ton, ti - ti - ton,  ton.

li - re, li - re,  ti - ti -ton li - re,  ti - ti -ton li - re,

In addition to the fixed forms, the rondeau and the virelai, Ivrea also contains four examples of the *chace*, a form based upon canon, where a second voice repeats after a short time interval a melody begun by the first voice. The name seems to derive from the French, *chasse*, meaning a hunt; the term is most appropriate for certain pieces, for their texts describe hunting scenes and include the sounds of the hunters and the dogs. In a musical sense, the *chace* is a chase, with one voice rushing after the other. This same type of composition, with the same connotations, is also to be found in Italy, under a similar designation, *caccia*.

The technique of the secular song as found in Ivrea resembles strongly the technique already seen in certain of the Mass Ordinary settings, those in which the emphasis is upon the upper voice, the lower ones being used as an instrumental support. The tenor is evidently inferior in interest, although superficially it often resembles tenor writing as seen in the motet. The contratenor is not limited to a simple filling in of the space between the tenor and the uppermost voice; instead, as in the Ordinary settings, it may cross the tenor and assume the place of the lowest voice. Without a designation within the source, it would often be difficult to determine which voice is the tenor. As an example of the style, we give the opening of "Amis tout doux" ("Such sweet friends") from Ivrea (Example 7-5, p. 142).

The simple beginnings of attention to secular forms as individual entities were to develop into a full-blown repertoire by the end of the fourteenth century, for later sources indicate more and more the rising interest in them. While in Ivrea there are but 15 secular works out of 81, in later manuscripts the proportion becomes higher; in the Chantilly source, to be discussed more fully later, out of 113 compositions there are but 13 motets. The other 100 pieces are secular forms—ballades, rondeaux, and virelais. Within the manuscript, there is a clear division of categories, for the motets, significantly enough, are found at the end of the volume grouped together in one unit; all are isorhythmic.

**EXAMPLE 7-5.**

## GUILLAUME DE MACHAUT

As a symbol of the spirit of the French Ars Nova, no better figure can be found than that of Guillaume de Machaut (1300?–1377?), for he summarizes within his life and work the spirit of the age; as one of the outstanding musicians of all time, he ranks with such other composers as Josquin, Palestrina, Bach, and Beethoven, in that he synthesizes the best of his own time. Viewing matters historically, one senses a progressive rise up to the works of Machaut, with a subsequent falling off in inspiration and in balance between form and feeling; Machaut is a peak between two valleys.

Machaut was born in Champagne of a noble family and, after taking orders, became the secretary of John of Luxembourg, King of Bohemia, in 1323. As part of King John's entourage, he followed his master on various military campaigns, in Silesia, Poland, and Lithuania. After 1330, still attached to John, he received successively benefits in various churches of France, in Verdun, Arras, Reims, and St.-Quentin; he was not required to be present in any of these places but, as was often the case at the time, was given the positions as rewards for his services, with consequent financial benefits. With the death of John at the battle of Crécy, Machaut turned to his daughter, whose husband was later to become John II of France. By 1349, when he had entered the employ of Charles, King of Navarre, his reputation was such that he was the intimate of kings and nobles; his works from this date show a close connection to royal circles. Although attached to the courts of Bohemia and Navarre, his principal residence after 1340 was in Reims, where he received visits from both the future Charles V of France and the Duke of Bar in 1361 and 1363. After 1364, he was, for a time, in the employ of Pierre de Lusignan, King of Cyprus, an area to become of cultural distinction at the beginning of the following century; he also had some connections with Amédée of Savoy, sending him a manuscript of his works in 1371. Little is known of his last years, and even the year of his death is not completely certain.

Machaut's life reflects the secularization of the century, for, although a cleric, his career was spent in secular circles; his connections to the Church were at best tenuous, although his main source of income was as beneficiary of various religious posts. As secretary to one of the most active kings of the time, he had the opportunity to come in contact with almost every major court and with the most cultivated societies of his time. For these circles, he produced poetry and music in about equal proportions, working for most of his life for one noble patron or another. The comparative profusion of sources containing Machaut's work is, in part, due to this situation, for he had the custom of having manuscripts prepared, under his supervision, for presentation to his noble patrons and friends.

The emphasis in Machaut's musical output is upon the secular, although there are a few religious compositions. Speaking first of the motet and its 23 examples, 15 are French double motets on profane subjects, two are mixed, with texts in both Latin and French, and the remaining six are Latin double motets; only two of these last have purely liturgical connections. Isorhythm is present in the tenors of nearly all of these, with isometric elements in the motetus and triplum as an accompanying feature. The tenors are drawn from all manner of sources, chant melodies and secular songs alike, although the sources of many tenors are still to be finally identified. In style, these works are well within the tradition established by de Vitry, but they show a variety and skill not found in those of the older master. Equality of imperfect and perfect mensurations is now wholly achieved, with no preference for one or the other.

The largest group of compositions is based on the secular forms, the lai, virelai, rondeau, and ballade. In these, Machaut shows his close relationship to the trouvère tradition, for many of these works are composed monophonically in much the same manner as in the past. Of the 19 lais, 16 are monophonic; 2 of the remaining 3, in three voices, utilize the canonic technique of the *chace*, while the third, for two voices, uses even-numbered lines as counterpoint to the preceding odd-numbered ones. Machaut was the last to compose lais, which were rapidly falling out of favor. Contemporary sources that contain other items by Machaut almost never contain lais, suggesting that their day of popularity had come to an end.

To a certain extent, the same situation may be seen in the virelais, for 25 of the 33 composed by Machaut are also monophonic; the remaining 8 are for two voices. This was, however, a form that was not to disappear, for its popularity remained high during the following century. The reasons for its neglect, and the neglect of the lai as well, may indeed rest on the general disappearance of monophonic music. To some degree, in these two areas Machaut looks back to the *Roman de Fauvel;* one of his lais is in fact directly connected to the *Roman.*

With the rondeaux and ballades, the evident interest is in polyphonic treatment, for all of the 22 rondeaux and 41 of the 42 ballades are so composed. The greatest number are for three voices, but there are many for two and a small number for four. Most are soloistic in character, with one voice accompanied instrumentally, but there are two triple ballades, with separate texts in all three voices. Of the rondeaux, the most fascinating is the "Ma fin est mon commencement," a superb example of *crab canon;* in it, all three voices proceed to the middle of the composition and then return to the beginning by repeating the material sung, but in reverse order.

Machaut's major religious work is the Mass for four voices, once thought to have been composed for the coronation of Charles V of France in 1364. Some scholars now date the work after 1337 and suggest that it was written for Notre Dame at Reims; others take the title "La Messe de Nostre Dame," found at its beginning in one source, as merely denoting that it is a Votive Mass in honor of the Blessed Virgin Mary. Regardless of the occasion for its composition, it is unique in the fourteenth century, for not only is it the only Ordinary setting known definitely to have been made by one man, but it is a complete setting, including not only the normal five sections but also an "Ite missa est." In style, it summarizes the advances made earlier, for its six movements include technical elements of all kinds. The Kyrie, Sanctus, and Agnus use tenors taken from plainchant, the Kyrie drawing on Mass IV (*LU,* 25), the Sanctus and Agnus on Mass XVII (*LU,* 61–62). Because of their lengthy texts, the Gloria and Credo use the conductus-like style already noted in Ivrea, but with an imagination and sureness not found there.

The degree of intellectual complexity shown in the Kyrie, Sanctus, and Agnus is quite high, for all three are governed by the principles of isorhythm and isometry, which not only influence the shape of the tenor and contratenor but also occasionally have impact on the motetus and triplum. In the Kyrie, for example, the tenor is completely isorhythmic, with *taleae* of increasing lengths; the first *talea* for each of the four movements is shown in Example 7-6.

**EXAMPLE 7-6.**

Comparison of the lengths of these four *taleae* shows the mathematical foundation of their structure, for they stand in unit length as 4–7–8–14; the *talea* of the third section is twice as long as that of the first, that of the fourth twice that of the second. The rhythmic coincidence of the opening bars of the first and second, and the third and fourth, is of equal significance. In the contratenor, also isorhythmic, the *talea* of the first section, with some small variation, is twelve units, of the second seven, of the third eight, and of the fourth fourteen; thus in the main we find a permutation of the tenor's structure. The motetus and triplum, while not in strict isometry, show its impact, for both are unified by rhythmic repetitions almost in the manner of a *talea,* not only by figures recurring in the same section but also by some appearing in several. Rhythmic identity and repetition, however, are not the only techniques of unification. Short melodic motives crop up again and again, almost in the manner of the Notre Dame formulae of a century earlier. The same procedures may be found in both the Sanctus and Agnus.

While the Gloria and Credo are in a conductus-like style, with no uses of isorhythm as a foundation in the tenor or elsewhere, a strong sense of unity derives from a similar use of formulae; a particularly obvious one is a short descending line in the triplum, often appearing near the close of one of the small sections into which these movements are divided. A second, found in both the Gloria and Credo, is a short transitional unit for tenor and contratenor that leads from the end of one section to the next. A significant feature of the Gloria is the emphasis on the two appearances of the words "Jesu Christe" in this movement; in both places stress is given them by their being set in block chords in maximae, notes twice as long as any others in the body of the composition.

Full analysis of the Mass is impossible here; our goal has been only to suggest something of the greatness of Machaut's ability to organize musical thoughts in an intellectual, complex way. The student who makes even a surface examination of the techniques employed in this work can hardly fail to understand why Machaut has become, in the eyes of today's musicians, one of the major figures of the past who still has meaning for our own time. His impact on Stravinsky, as in the latter's *Mass*, was both profound and germinating; and we have already noted that the laying out of *color* and *talea* in isorhythm has many correspondences with the techniques involved in composing a serial work.

One other religious work by Machaut deserves mention, the "David Hoquetus," for three voices. The tenor is based on a chant used previously by Perotin in his "Alleluia-Nativitas" (mentioned earlier); it has been suggested that Machaut's composition was designed to complete that of his great predecessor. The tenor is completely isorhythmic, while the upper two voices are written in hoquet. This technique had its greatest vogue during the thirteenth century, although it still forms one of the basic characteristics of the motet of the Ars Nova. (Example 7-5, in measures 6, 11, and 14, includes hoquet in the upper two voices.)

With Machaut, the energy of the French Ars Nova was at an end. As the last composer of the century to achieve a balance between all the elements of musical technique, Machaut represents the drive begun during the late thirteenth century to free musicians from the often restricting partnership with philosophy, to find a liberty of expression not possible before. With the last quarter of the century, the balance shown in Machaut's works was to disappear, in favor of emphasis upon the complicated and the overblown, upon notational detail and mensural intricacy.

Paris, Bibliothèque Nationale, Fr. 1585, folio 283 verso and 284 recto. The music here is the opening of the Gloria of the Mass by Guillaume de Machaut. Each of the four voices can be distinguished by the large initials of the opening, "Et in terra."

What had been a clear leadership on the part of French musicians was to disappear before a new clarity of goal and a new sense of the appropriate on the part of composers of other areas.

A sign of the approaching fall of French practice was the rise of a school of musicians in Italy, an area previously known only as an outlying artistic province of France. Even though it was not to maintain a reputation for long, the Italian school did give signs of the possibility to consider musical practices from other angles than those stemming from the greatest of medieval centers for music, Notre Dame de Paris. It is this new art of Italy to which we must now turn.

## BIBLIOGRAPHICAL NOTES

The music of the Fauvel manuscript and the complete works of Philippe de Vitry and Guillaume de Machaut can be found in the first three volumes of Leo Schrade, *Polyphonic Music of the Fourteenth Century* (Monaco: Oiseau Lyre, 1956–   ). Other major sources have been published by the American Institute of Musicology in Rome; these include Willi Apel, *French Secular Compositions of the Fourteenth Century* (3 vol., 1970–1972); Hanna Stäblein-Harder, *Fourteenth-Century Mass Music in France* (1962); and Nigel E. Wilkins, *A 14th Century Repertory from the Codex Reina* (1964).

Many of the critical Latin treatises from this period have been published by the American Institute of Musicology; a partial list includes volumes by Philippe de Vitry, Johannes de Muris, Johannes de Boen, and many anonymous writers. De Vitry's *Ars Nova* has been translated into English by Leon Plantinga, *Journal of Music Theory*, V (1961).

The literature on the period is found primarily in journal articles, many of them in *Musica Disciplina*. The major authorities writing in English are Gilbert Reaney and Ursula Günther. In addition to his many articles, Reaney is the author of an extremely useful separate study, *Guillaume de Machaut* (London: Oxford University Press, 1971). Günther's article, "The 14th-Century Motet and its Development," *Musica Disciplina*, XII (1958), is also valuable, as is Willi Apel's "The Development of French Secular Music During the Fourteenth Century," *Musica Disciplina*, XXVII (1973). Stäblein-Harder has published a separate study of the music she has edited (see above); this was brought out by the American Institute of Musicology under the same title. Earlier studies by Leo Schrade, in *Acta Musicologica, Journal of the American Musicological Society,* and the *Revue Belge de Musicologie,* are still of value, for they discuss the material contained in his editions and add much supplementary information. A collection of essays and of discussions carried on at Wégimont,

Belgium, in 1965 should be consulted, particularly the essays by Schrade and Apel. The title is *Les Colloques de Wégimont, II-1955, L'Ars Nova (Bibliothèque de la Faculté de Philosophie et Lettres de l'Université de Liège, Fasc. CXLIX)* (Paris: "Les Belles Lettres," 1959). Although not dealing directly with musical problems, J. Huizinga, *The Waning of the Middle Ages* (London: Arnold, 1924; many later re-editions, including paperback), gives a magnificent picture of the times; his discussion of Machaut, particularly his place as a poet, is especially of value.

# EIGHT

# THE ITALIAN ARS NOVA

Little is known about the development of composed polyphony in Italy to 1300, although it is obvious from inspection of the earliest preserved compositions, from around 1330, that Italians had already a fairly extensive experience in its writing; these early works show an orginality and skill not possible in first attempts. While French influence is clear, with characteristics of thirteenth-century conductus in some of these Italian compositions, there is also an individuality that indicates not only a complete assimilation of the French approaches but the forging of a peculiarly Italian style, something that could only have taken place over a fairly long period.

Further evidence of a maturity in style is the high degree of perfection and individualism seen in Italian notational methods at the beginning of the fourteenth century. These are described in the *Pomerium* of Marchettus of Padua (late thirteenth century–early fourteenth century), written between 1321 and 1326, a treatise clearly outlining the notational

practices of Italian composers and the differences between their procedures and those of French musicians. The methods described in the
*Pomerium* are not completely original, for they are derivations of the
French system in vogue during the third quarter of the thirteenth century, that of Pierre de la Croix. The Italian derivations have a sufficiently
high level of complexity and comprehensiveness to suggest strongly a
somewhat lengthy period of previous experimentation and development.

Early examples of Italian polyphony are nearly all secular works,
although there are a few processional compositions for two voices. This
emphasis on secular polyphony is a general characteristic of the Italian
Ars Nova, for little polyphonic music seems to have been composed for
liturgical purposes. Instead, the principal function of the composer was
the provision of music for social occasions of all kinds, music that could be
used to heighten the enjoyment of life. Descriptions of social activities of
the times as given in Boccaccio's *Decameron* (1353) and the *Paradiso degli
Alberti* (1425?) of Giovanni da Prato indicate that music was an integral
part of Italian social life and that it was not performed solely by professional musicians but also by gifted amateurs.

This audience was not interested in the technicalities of counterpoint and rhythm so much enjoyed by the French. Melodic improvisation
played a large role in Italian music, with much attention paid to the
simultaneous improvisation of both words and music; this technique is
still to be found in the late fifteenth century, for Baccio Ugolini, of the
court of Lorenzo il Magnifico, was highly esteemed for his abilities in this
difficult art. Such a stress on melody as a major constituent of music gives
to Italian compositions of the Ars Nova a completely different orientation
from the French, for, instead of the tenor's being a strong foundation
above which the other parts are composed, the uppermost melody, that
with the poetic text, is preeminent and acts as a generator of the lower
lines. With Italian compositions, the tenor and contratenor are supports
of a melody that is itself an elaboration and ornamentation of an originally simpler line.

The high position of improvisation was not peculiar to secular
music; it accounts also for the lack of attention given by Italian musicians
to the composition of sacred polyphony. Improvisation supplied all the
needs for polyphony within the church, leaving little necessity for composed polyphony. Understanding as did their French contemporaries that
polyphony was an ideal means by which to enhance a particular service,
the Italians introduced it where appropriate, but did not go to the point
of elaborating it into anything more than ornamentation of the given
plainchant by adding to it improvised note-against-note counterpoint.
Development of organum and discantus styles in the manner of St.
Martial was completely foreign to Italy. A description of how to improvise

a counterpoint of more than one note to another does not appear in Italy until the late fourteenth century and, even then, this new technique does not seem to have been generally adopted. Within the fourteenth century proper, there are but a handful of composed polyphonic religious works, showing nothing like the attention paid to this category by French composers of both thirteenth and fourteenth centuries. Even composers part of a religious establishment, men such as the Florentines of the mid-fourteenth century, concentrate their efforts on the production of secular music to the neglect of the sacred. With the use of simple improvisation as a practical solution to the problem of providing polyphony for the services, interest in the development of sacred music stopped.

This practical attitude toward music is further reflected in the theoretical treatises of the time, for the vast majority of them are directed toward practical goals. Those collections of treatises that were part of every cathedral library were severely practical in their approaches, for they include only those items that are of value and necessity to the performer in the choir. Every one of them includes at least one work on improvisation, some coming from centuries earlier; Guido's *Micrologus* is an almost constant constituent of these collections. To show the emphasis, Ugolino's *Declaratio*, one of the last great speculative works, is found complete in only two sources; its practical sections, however, particularly that on plainchant, appear as excerpts in eight others. Music, to Italians, was essentially a skill of producing beautiful sounds.

This is not to say that there was no production of speculative material, for the first work of Marchettus of Padua, the *Lucidarium* from approximately 1317–1318, is an excellent example of the species. Yet it was not followed by many others, and the remaining theoretical treatises of the Ars Nova come only after the end of the century, those by Johannes de Ciconia (1340?–1411) and Prosdocimus de Beldemandis (1380?–1428). Between the *Lucidarium* and the works of these men, there is a giant gap in which nothing new was produced, reliance probably being placed upon treatises of an earlier age recopied into new manuscripts.

Within Italian speculative treatises there is not the clear reliance upon authority that is so characteristic of French sources. Marchettus, for example, shows something of the Italian tendency toward pure practicality in his discussion of semitones, for, by setting up three of different size, he allows a type of chromaticism that is completely impossible in the pure Pythagorean system then in vogue. He also makes reference to the judgment of the ear as to dissonance and consonance, saying that a dissonance is that which is required by the ear to move to a consonance.

The reason for the lack of emphasis upon the speculative treatise may lie in the fact that, unlike Paris, where the university was strong in the liberal arts and was, in fact, primarily devoted to this type of curriculum, Italian universities specialized in other fields, ones in which music played no such great role. The University of Bologna, the oldest in Italy, was primarily known for the study of medicine, while that of Padua, dating from 1222, emphasized law; only in 1399 was there a separate faculty of arts established at Padua. While music surely must have played some part in the educational scheme at both schools, it could have received nothing like the attention that it got at Paris, where the cathedral school and the university were in close contact. The works of both Ciconia and Prosdocimus reflect the needs of the newly introduced faculty of arts at the University of Padua and were probably inspired by this elevation of the liberal arts; both men were in Padua at the time, and Prosdocimus was a member of its faculty.

The separation of philosophical and practical musical education in Italy caused some problems for musicians there. While it was possible to acquire much knowledge in the special fields, it seems to have been understood that Paris remained the major center for the true education of a *musicus*. There is evidence that many Italian musicians left their homeland to study at Paris because their native universities were not quite adequate; we read in a necrology of Florentine Carmelites that, in 1341, one of their brethren, an organist and cantor named Bartholomeus Duccini, died in Burgundy on his way to Paris as a student.

To summarize, we may say that Italy, in music as in the visual arts, was the first area to feel the impact of the new spirit that has been called the Renaissance. Its orientation toward music was not that of the Middle Ages, for its designated function for music was as a sensual entertainment for a secular minded society. For these circles, the major areas of study within music were those of almost pure practicality, with little reference to any form of speculative foundation. The sole criterion was the beauty of the music itself as determined by its physical characteristics, its impact upon the ear, without great consideration of its place within a speculative scheme. To Italians, music had become a true fine art, with only small remnants of the speculative remaining as vestiges of a vanished age.

## THE FORMS

Within the secular music of the Italian Ars Nova, three forms were intensely cultivated; all had some relation to French models.

During the first part of the period, major attention was given to the *madrigal*, a form comparable to the ballade in that there are two sections of music, the first repeated; the second section, called the *ritornello* and acting in the manner of a refrain, is in a different meter, thus making a clear contrast against the opening material. Although both carry the same name, the fourteenth-century madrigal has nothing to do with that of the sixteenth; the later form did not develop from the earlier one.

The madrigal was of Veneto-Lombardic origin, from the North of Italy, and was cultivated as a monophonic form in the late thirteenth century. In its beginnings, it seems to have been a rustic manifestation, a song of love of the type performed by shepherds and peasants. When taken over by more sophisticated circles, it was treated polyphonically, yet retained in its text something of its pastoral beginnings. Writing in 1332, the Paduan, Antonio da Tempo, emphasizes this background, even suggesting that the rhythms as well as the subject matter of the poetry should try to retain the rustic feeling.

Madrigals are found in both two and three voices and in combination with the *caccia*, that canonic treatment already seen in the French *chace*. An anonymous Venetian theorist of around 1330 suggests that one voice, the tenor, should be in longae, while the upper voice or voices should move in minimae. This writer indicates that a clear distinction was already being made between Italian and French styles, for he speaks of an Italian and a French manner, the latter quite useful, so he says, at the end of a section.

While many earlier madrigals, particularly those in two voices, reflect these directions, not all are so simply composed. Even those that come from the Vatican manuscript, Rossi 215, the source of our earliest examples, do not always follow these prescriptions; some show an effort on the part of the composer to make the lower voice more interesting, either by giving it interludes in short values or by allowing it to move in the same rhythmic patterns as the upper voice, with many short notes. Even where this involves a clear difference in movement between the two voices, both sing the text together. Examples 8-1 and 8-2 give the opening measures of the two madrigals, "Chiamando un'astorella" and "Su la rivera."

The later madrigal, for two and three voices, goes beyond this simple technique, for, in some two-voice works, there are short imitative passages and also hoquet. We find again a desire to make the lower voice something more than a simple support. Even in compositions for three voices, where the tenor, the lowest voice, is much in accord with the directions given by our anonymous theorist, there are occasional passages that remind one of conductus, where all three voices move together on the same syllables. One may also find contrast between the first and second sections made by number of voices as well as by a change of rhythm, the ritornello often dropping to but two as opposed to the preceding section

EXAMPLE 8-1.

EXAMPLE 8-2.

with three. Something of the three-voice technique may be seen in Example 8-3, the opening of "Nel prato pien de fiori," where even the tenor is part of the contrapuntal web.

The *caccia* is, like its French counterpart, purely canonic in technique, with strict imitation. Although there are many works in two voices, like the French models, the Italians generally leaned to three-voice compositions. The third voice, a tenor, is not normally part of the canonic structure, but acts as a support in long notes to the rhythmic activity of the upper two. There are exceptions to this, however, such as in the "De' dimmi tu" of Francesco Landini, where it is the uppermost voice that

**EXAMPLE 8-3.**

stands outside the canon, only the lower two being involved in the strict imitation; this work is not a pure example of the form, for it is a mixture of the caccia and madrigal. The ritornello is in triple canon, the tenor entering at an octave below and the middle voice at a fourth below the opening uppermost voice. Example 8-4 gives the opening bars of the ritornello.

Texts of the caccia often include realistic elements such as shouts, bird calls, hunting cries, and various kinds of exclamations. Their subject matter is often humorous and may even descend to the licentious. The general effect is one of appeal to a high social level, one that understood the technical dexterity needed to compose the form as well as appreciated the way in which the composer could emphasize the textual

**EXAMPLE 8-4.**

meanings. In spirit, the caccia is quite close to many of the secular pieces then popular in France, such as the "Or sus" mentioned in the previous chapter.

The preserved sources of Italian Trecento (thirteenth-century) music have left us approximately 175 madrigals and 25 cacce, with some 420 examples of the third form cultivated in the period, the *ballata.* This should not be taken to imply that the ballata is the most important form of the three, but merely that the madrigal, the major form of the early part of the century, declined in interest under the impact of the ballata, which

was the form most cultivated toward the close of the period. Although
the madrigal continued to be composed, it no longer held as much interest and thereby suffered a certain neglect.

   The form of the ballata is that of the French virelai and, in the
beginning, was a monophonic dance work, as its name suggests; we have
no preserved examples of these types, although there are some monophonic ballate found in the Rossi manuscript, but with texts that imply
nothing of the dance. The classic period of the ballata, after 1365, is that
in which the form has become polyphonic, for two or three voices. As in
its French equivalent there are but two sections of music: the first for the
refrain (*ripresa*) and the third and fourth lines of the strophe (the *volta*);
the second for the first and second lines of the strophe (the *piedi*) and
sung twice often with first and second endings (the *aperto* and *chiuso*).
The form thus is, in musical terms, an ABBAA, the two B's serving for
the *piedi*, the A's serving for the *ripresa* and the *volta*. Example 8-5 is the
beginning of the ballata, "L'alma mie piange," by Francesco Landini, as
transcribed from the version found in Paris, Bib. Nat., ital. 568.

**EXAMPLE 8-5.**

   In this short excerpt, one may notice the importance of the rhythmic interest in the lower two parts through contrast achieved by hoquet
(or hocket) and irregular entries. Further, the penultimate syllable is
extended by a fairly long melisma; in the complete ballata, as in many
others, this kind of extension is customary at the end of every line, something like a vocalise defining the formal structure of the text.

   Little attention was paid by Italian composers to motet form, either
to motets of the past or to the form as a vehicle for their own composition.
Only one thirteenth-century motet seems to have been copied into Italian

sources of the Trecento and but a few were composed during the early part of the century. Something of the attitude of Italian musicians toward the form can be seen in the "Lux purpurata—Diligite justiciam" of Jacopo da Bologna, composed about 1342 for Luchino Visconti in Milan. Superficially it resembles the French motet, but closer inspection reveals some characteristic Italian traits. The free-composed tenor is neither isorhythmic nor isometric; its values are arranged with no discernible plan and there appears to be neither *color* nor *talea*. The upper voices have intimations of isometry, but it is not carried through. One gets the impression that Jacopo was trying to imitate the characteristics of the French motet, but without thoroughly understanding the principles involved. As with secular works, the emphasis is on the uppermost voice, the tenor acting as a support, not a generator. The style is that of a three-voice ballata, but with the bi-textuality of the motet.

A similar neglect is true of settings of the Ordinary of the Mass. One nearly complete Ordinary, found in the Paris manuscript just mentioned, contains all portions except the Kyrie and adds a Benedicamus. Like most of the Ordinaries found in French sources, the various sections are by different composers, the Gloria and Agnus by Ser Gherardello, the Credo by Bartolino da Firenze, and the Sanctus by Lorenzo da Firenze; the Benedicamus is anonymous. Isolated settings of the Gloria, Credo, and Sanctus are found in other sources, with one manuscript (London, British Museum, add. 29987) including a Sanctus and a Benedictus, both of which are troped in Italian; significantly, both these tropes are written in the poetic form of the madrigal.

In style, these Mass movements from the Paris manuscript are closely allied to the madrigal. The text is simultaneously declaimed by all voices, although the lowest one is normally without ornament or embellishment. Imitation may appear in short sections, but there is no attempt to use this technique in more than fragmentary form. Hoquet appears rarely. The overall form is derived from the breaking up of the text into small bits, these short sections then being set as units, without effort to make one flow into the other. Even in those Ordinary chants with little text, the same desire to make of the piece a mosaic of little bits is in evidence; the anonymous Benedicamus setting has five of these, the longest extending to fourteen measures of transcription, the shortest to just six, all of this within a total length of fifty measures. One of these sections is given in Example 8-6 as an example of the approach. The use of dissonance on weak beats, particularly as in the seventh bar, points up the composer's emphasis on horizontal elements, the vertical harmonic relations taking a secondary role; the two upper parts are spun-out melismata, almost like textless vocalises.

Modern Italian scholars insist upon the continuity of an Italian

EXAMPLE 8-6.

musical tradition centered about the exposition of the beauty of the voice; no matter the subject or the period, their studies always emphasize this point, as, in speaking of the great figures of the Ars Nova, they frequently refer to Verdi and Puccini as the inheritors of a great past. While such statements may seem too sweeping at first glance, there is much truth in what they say, for Italian composers of the Trecento are clearly most interested in the conduct of the uppermost voice, treating it in the manner of a coloratura line, almost to the exclusion of individuality in the other voices. One may contrast French and Italian methods by suggesting that the French worked up from the tenor, while the Italians worked down from the uppermost voice. To Italian composers, the tenor was that voice that filled in and supported, acting as a neutral background for the elaborate line or lines above it. To hear a caccia in three voices is a convincing demonstration, for, against the slow moving tenor, the upper voices entwine and embroider their elaborate lines in much the same way that gold and silver threads make vivid the picture within a tapestry whose basic tone is grey or brown.


## SCHOOLS AND COMPOSERS


Until the middle of the fourteenth century, most compositional activity was concentrated in the northern part of Italy, with Milan, Venice, Verona, Rimini, and Padua acting as major centers. Although many composers of the time were born elsewhere, they eventually gravitated to one of these cities, particularly during the rule of certain musically inclined princes such as Mastino della Scala, tyrant of Verona from 1329 to 1351; Giovanni da Cascia and Jacopo da Bologna were both at one time in his service. Jacopo is believed to have been the teacher of Landini; he did produce one theoretical work, a discussion of notation.

After the middle of the century, the musical center of gravity shifted South, to Tuscany and in particular to Florence. This city, perhaps better known for its humanistic leadership in the late 1400's under Lorenzo il Magnifico, was already an artistic center in the fourteenth century. As the city of Dante, Boccaccio, and Petrarch, to name only three major figures of a large group of distinguished and talented writers, it had already shown the burgeonings in literature of the full Renaissance to come. Its musical leadership during the same period was of equal distinction and represents the height of achievement within the Italian Ars Nova.

Of the many composers working in and around Florence in the third quarter of the century, the greatest figure is that of Francesco Landini (1335?–1397), a musician-poet comparable in his versatility and genius to Guillaume de Machaut in France at the same time. Blinded at an early age from the aftereffects of smallpox, Landini became the leading organist of the city and was known particularly for his abilities on the small portative organ. His extra-musical talents were also highly appreciated, for he was a part of the intellectual circles around the University of Florence that included Salutati. As a poet, he wrote many of the texts to which he set his music and, in addition, composed a Latin poem in defense of the logic of William of Occam.

Landini's outstanding position was recognized by his contemporaries, for his output makes up about one-fourth the repertoire of the Italian Ars Nova that is preserved, its high place indicated by the great number of sources into which it was copied. Unlike the works of most other Florentine musicians of the time, which appear only in sources from Tuscany proper, Landini's compositions appear also in manuscripts from other parts of Italy; from the evidence of these sources plus certain poetic texts, it is probable that Landini had many close connections with the North, particularly Venice. It is possible that he may have visited that city many times, to display his skill as a performer and composer.

Of Landini's 154 preserved compositions, the vast majority are ballate, 91 for two and 42 for three voices, with 8 others in double-text versions, for two and for three. The remainder of the output is divided between the madrigal, with 9 for two and 2 for three voices, and the caccia, with but 2 examples. It is also believed that he wrote motets, for there are surviving records to show that at least 5 were commissioned; these, however, have been lost.

Florence, Biblioteca Medicea-Laurenziana, Palat. 87, folio 7 verso. This
highly illuminated page gives a part of Jacopo da Bologna's madrigal,
"Sotto l'imperio." The miniature is presumably a portrait of Jacopo, with
his name given in alternating blue and red letters at the upper edge of
the page.

Most of these compositions are preserved in one of the more elaborate manuscripts of the early fifteenth century, the *Squarcialupi Codex*, so named because it was at one time the property of Antonio Squarcialupi, the organist of the Florence cathedral during the time of Lorenzo. Although the manuscript is not one of the more accurate sources for the music which it contains, it is most extensively illuminated and contains among its miniatures a portrait of Landini playing the portative. It seems to have been put together as an attempt to collect the works of the outstanding Florentine musicians of the Ars Nova; the music of Landini occupies almost half the volume's 352 pieces. From the format of the book, its use of vellum, and the emphasis on sheer beauty of illumination, it is evident that the codex was never intended to be part of a practical musician's working library but was rather to be an ornament in the private collection of a book lover, a manifestation of the steadily increasing desire of Italian upper classes to picture themselves as culturally distinguished.

Unlike the music of Machaut, Landini's works show the Italian concentration upon the voice, for the greater part of his compositions are vocally oriented. The overwhelming majority of the ballate, for instance, are in the form of the unaccompanied duet, with 82 of the 91 two-voice examples being for this medium. Within the three-voice ballate, one, "Perche di novo," is a triple ballata, with different texts for all three voices; on the other hand, most of this group is written for vocal solo with accompaniment for two instruments, suggesting some French influence. The nine two-voice madrigals are also all vocal duets, the two three-voice ones vocal trios. "Musica son" is a triple madrigal, with individual texts for all three voices. The madrigal "Si dolce," a terzet, is of particular interest, for it shows the influence of French isorhythmic procedures. Here, the tenor is completely isorhythmic, with isometry in the two upper parts. "Adiu, adiu" is completely French in that it is a virelai and, unlike any other of Landini's works, has a French text.

Landini's handling of melismata implies a strong feeling for vocal technique, with a limpidness of flow matched by no other composer of his time. Penultimate syllables are often emphasized with sweeping melodic insertions, leading finally into graceful cadences. To match the smoothness of individual line, there is also a harmonic clarity and avoidance of dissonance in contrapuntal movement; harsh sequences of parallel seconds and sevenths, as well as fifths and octaves, are no longer constant parts of the polyphonic web, and triadic formations are quite common, except at cadence points where the traditional perfect intervals are found. The overall effect is one of suavity and easy flow, typically Italian. To show something of this, Example 8-7 gives the opening measures of the two-voice ballata, "Se pronto," from the version in the *Squarcialupi Codex*.

**EXAMPLE 8-7.**

Within Landini's work, there is already evidence of considerable influence from France, not only in the introduction of certain peculiarly French features of rhythmic complication and formal construction, but within the notation itself; the pure Italian notational practices of the early Trecento have begun to be displaced in favor of methods whose details had been perfected under the impact of French musical style. After Landini, in the latter part of the fourteenth century and the beginning of the fifteenth, there is more and more of a turn to French models, not only in notation and rhythm but also in the forms themselves and the language used. The madrigal then disappears almost completely and, although there is still some concentration upon the ballata, many composers turn to the ballade and virelai, composing both to French texts. Before, French characteristics had been impressed on Italian works; now it is the reverse, for these compositions are French pieces with an Italian accent. Native Italian musical art was not to recover for more than a century from the initial impact of French practice, remaining submerged under successive waves of non-Italian domination until the beginning of the sixteenth century.

## ITALIAN NOTATION

As we stated earlier, Italian notation in its purest form is a derivation from the methods employed by Pierre de la Croix; it has been suggested that he was an Italian who brought his ideas to Paris. In essence, the system is based on the division of the brevis into from two to twelve parts, with a verbal description indicating the number of semibreves to the brevis and their internal groupings; in practice, the describing word or words were abbreviated, as, for example, *.n.*, meaning *novenaria*, with the brevis divided into three groups of three semibreves each or nine in all. Within the musical line, those groups making up the value of a brevis were separated one from the other by points of division, acting in many ways like modern bar lines. To indicate values other than the standard semibrevis, tails of various kinds were added, both up and down, to the oblique, with and without flags; the basic note shapes could also be altered, for, to indicate shades of mensural meaning, they could be written as solid or hollow notes in either black or red. Italian notation from its inception could thus notate many things not easily possible in the system of de Vitry and de Muris, but it had one inherent weakness, namely, that its complications were restricted to the brevis grouping; no syncopation was possible, and rhythmic intricacies could not be carried from one group to another.

With increasing French influence around the middle of the fourteenth century, Italian notation began to adapt certain features of the system employed by musicians of France; Italian interest in the possibilities of syncopation as exploited by the French forced revision of their system. Italian nomenclature was retained for the various kinds of mensural groupings, but their meaning and notation were now close to the French system involving modus, tempus, and prolatio. This notation, a mixture of both French and Italian elements, is found normally in works by composers of the later school; almost all the compositions of Landini are written in this mixed manner. Certain works of this mid-century may be found notated differently in various sources, showing a transition away from

Italian methods to those of France; while the tonal effect of the two versions is the same, the visual appearance is quite different.

By the end of the century, the victory of French notation was complete. An anonymous treatise of the late fourteenth century, written in Italian for a Florentine convent of nuns, gives nothing but the rules for French notational procedures, without mention of Italian methods. Prosdocimus de Beldemandis, in his two treatises on notation written about the beginning of the fifteenth century, pleads the advantages of the Italian manner in a most persuasive language, but it is evident, even to him, that it is a lost cause and that French notation has won the day. The style for which Italian notation was so fitting was no longer in existence and there was thus no reason for its retention.

## BIBLIOGRAPHICAL NOTES

For the student wishing to study the Italian Ars Nova in more detail, the most complete specialized bibliography is Viola L. Hagopian, *Italian Ars Nova Music* (2nd ed., Berkeley: University of California Press, 1973); Hagopian not only lists the pertinent material but epitomizes its content as well. In addition, she lists all composers of the period individually, giving sources for transcriptions of their works and an index to various secondary sources which discuss the composers. Among the available articles in English, Kurt von Fischer's "On the Technique, Origin, and Evolution of Italian Trecento Music," in *Musical Quarterly*, XLVII (1961), is of great value as a general discussion. His *Studien zur italienischen Musik des Trecento und frühen Quattrocento* (Bern: Haupt, 1956) is a list of works and their sources, arranged by form and text incipit. Special topics are discussed by Leonard Ellinwood, "Francesco Landini and his Music," in *Musical Quarterly*, XXII (1936), still useful in spite of its age, and the three volumes published under the general title, *L'Ars Nova italiana del Trecento* (Certaldo: Centro di studi sull'Ars Nova italiana del Trecento, 1962, 1968, 1970).

For the music, two major series are in the process of publication, the first edited by Nino Pirotta, *The Music of Fourteenth-Century Italy*, 5 vols. (Amsterdam: American Institute of Musicology, 1954– ), the second edited by W. Thomas Marrocco, *Polyphonic Music of the Fourteenth Century*, Vols. VI, VII, and VIII (Monaco: Editions de l'Oiseau-Lyre, 1967– ); the works of Landini are most easily accessible in Leo Schrade's edition, in Vol. IV of the latter series. Marrocco has also published the *Fourteenth-Century Italian Cacce* (2nd ed., Cambridge: Mediaeval Academy, 1961) and *Music of Jacopo da Bologna* (Berkeley: University of California Press, 1954). Other important sources include

Johannes Wolf and Hans Albrecht, eds., *Der Squarcialupi-Codex, Pal. 87 der Biblioteca Medicea Laurenziana zu Florenz* (Lippstadt: Kistner & Siegel, 1955) and Leonard Ellinwood, ed., *The Works of Francesco Landini* (Cambridge: Mediaeval Academy, 1939).

# NINE

# THE PASSING
# OF MEDIEVAL MUSIC

By the end of the fourteenth century, the decay of the medieval world and all it stood for was an accomplished fact, with ample evidence of the inability of its institutions to cope with the difficulties brought on by changing concepts of social organization and purpose. The Church, so long the acknowledged guide and director of man's activities on earth as preparation for his soul's eternal life in heaven, had, in spite of all its efforts, become a political weapon in the hands of ambitious kings. Its claims as the arbiter of all Christendom, with papal supremacy over all human affairs, were no longer taken seriously by those in power; the thesis of Marsiglio of Padua, announced in his *Defensor Pacis* of 1324, that kings were superior in secular affairs to any pope and that the Church was but one activity of the State, was well on its way toward general acceptance. Certainly the events of the time—the Great Schism, the revolt of the French clergy against the Avignonese Benedict XIII in 1398, the growing pressure from secular princes for the convening of a council to settle the problems of spiritual leadership—these and many others indicate the distance traveled since the days of Boniface VIII and his claims for papal primacy in all matters, sacred and secular.

National affairs were in no better condition, for political disruption was evident all over Europe. In France, governmental paralysis was endemic; with the accession of Charles VI in 1380, revolts of both commoners and nobles succeeded one upon the other; Charles's period of insanity led to intrigues and instability climaxed by outright civil war. In England, the situation was hardly better, for, under Richard II, only a short period in the middle of his reign could be called peaceful; his rule had begun with the Peasants' Revolt (1381) and closed with his forced abdication and imprisonment in 1399. Not until the time of Henry V, well into the fifteenth century, was there any real sense of direction. Italy too was politically confused, for most of the peninsula was involved in intermittent wars, the aftermath of the Guelf-Ghibelline rivalries of earlier times. Rome, no longer the sole center of European religious hegemony, was at a low point; Florence, although enjoying a surface prosperity, was soon to suffer a series of defeats in battle and failures of its financial houses that would topple them from their former position of distinction. In Milan, the death of Gian Galeazzo Visconti in 1402 opened a period of anarchy not to be closed until the tyranny of Francesco Sforza, beginning in 1447. Venice was the only stable city in all of Italy, but it had problems of trade and commerce that eventually led to a long series of expensive wars with the Turks, beginning in 1416. Germany, with knotty problems of succession and nationalism, was in continual turmoil; we have already mentioned the simultaneous presence of three Holy Roman Emperors.

With such a state of affairs, it can be no surprise that the music of the late fourteenth and early fifteenth centuries has little artistic validity or inspiration. An artistic situation in which the goals of a previous civilization and its social stability had been discarded, but which lacked the introduction of new ideals and functions or an established social order, could but lead to sterility and formalism, particularly in music, where the connections between form and function had, in medieval times, been so close. Feeling no aesthetic goal for his creations nor a secure place in a stable society, the composer of the closing years of the century retreated into technical complexity, with little more than this to distinguish his music. Little in the immediate future could be hoped for from those areas that had brought medieval music to its peak; just as Italian music had fallen before that of France, so did that of France give way before that of England and the Lowlands.

## FRANCE AT THE CLOSE OF THE ARS NOVA

The most significant document showing the decay of French music in the late fourteenth century is the Chantilly manuscript, copied in Florence during the fifteenth century but reflecting the musical situation in Southern France and Aragon during the latter part of the preceding century. Its 113 pieces indicate the changes in style and repertoire of the Ars Nova, with notational complexities suggesting that the source from which Chantilly was copied was designed to examine the sight-singing abilities of aspirants for employment within a royal chapel.

Within Chantilly, the preponderant place is given to the ballade, with 70 compositions, the overwhelming majority of them being for three voices. There are, in addition, 30 other works in the fixed forms, divided about equally between the rondeau and the virelai; 6 rondeaux are isometric. The volume closes with 13 isorhythmic motets, 9 for four voices and 4 for three voices. While several compositions date from a previous time, 4 coming from the earlier Ivrea manuscript and 13 by Machaut, the bulk of the manuscript contains music by composers of the last quarter of the century. While many of these men were clearly connected to the Papal Court at Avignon, some were part of such diverse locales as the Courts of the Duke of Lancaster, Gaston Phoebus, the Duke of Foix, John I and Martin I of Aragon, Charles V and Charles VI of France, and Jean, Duke of Berry. Many of these composers had careers extending well into the fifteenth century, for we find Johannes Cesaris and Gacien Reyneau, to name only two, still composing in the 1420's.

Within Chantilly, the evident stress is upon the secular, although a handful of works (two ballades, one virelai, and three motets) have sacred connotations; they are, however, without fixed liturgical position. Among the most interesting of the secular ballades in one by F. Andrieu, a lament on the death of Guillaume de Machaut in 1377(?), based on a text by Eustache Deschamps, the friend of Chaucer. Two other works, both isorhythmic motets, have texts based on lists of choir members, a type of work also found in other sources; one here is by John Aleyne, an Englishman, while the other is anonymous and lists singers within the Augustinian order at Florence. As additions of a later date to the manuscript, two works by M. Baude Cordier show something of the effort to make even the appearance of the music beautiful: one, "Belle, bonne, sage," is written in the shape of a heart, with the staves curving to form the outline; the other, "Tout par compas," is in a circular shape, a visual representation of the opening words of the text.

The outstanding characteristic of Chantilly is its notational complexity, seen in its use of all possible means of indicating mensural values. Not only are there the time signatures for tempus and prolatio suggested by de Vitry and de Muris, and note shapes in solid black, solid red, and hollow red, there are also many special directions for the correct realization of the composer's intent. Most of these indicate how the mensural signs are to be read, with specific directions for interpretation. Not all of these devices appear in every composition and, in many cases, there is no need for those that are used. Too often, the notational complexities have no other goal than that of being difficult to interpret; certain passages could easily have been written in a simpler manner, so the music itself seems but an excuse for piling notational complications upon one another. There are varying levels of complexity within the modern compositions of Chantilly, yet even the simplest of them are filled with syncopations and rhythmic intricacies that go far beyond anything known before. To give a sample of the kind of complication that can be found, we give the second half of the opening section of the ballade, "Se doit il plus" (Example 9-1), by Johannes de Alte Curie, an otherwise unknown composer.

**EXAMPLE 9-1.**

The opening, that part omitted in our example, is not overly filled with syncopation, with all three voices in the same 6/8 rhythm. At the point where the example begins, there is a new time signature given for the uppermost voice, while that for the lower two remains the same. While the tenor maintains a fairly even pace, the contratenor begins a series of syncopations not brought to rest until the cadence, where all voices begin a new mensuration. This closing section is typical of the late Ars Nova, for not only is there continuous syncopation of the duplum against the tenor, but there is also a rhythmic opposition between the lower two voices, based on eight eighths to the measure, against the triplum with its nine; the only constant element is the brevis, which fills the measure throughout and is always the same in duration. In the course of the composition, it is, however, divided into two groups of three (6/8), three groups of two (3/4), three groups of three (9/8), and four groups of two (4/4).

The emphasis on rhythmic oppositions and their notation is responsible for the introduction of time signatures indicated by numbers rather than by symbols; both works by M. Baude Cordier employ one or two numbers at the beginning of individual sections. The meaning of these numbers, however, is not that of today, but is a direction for the performer to make a new mensuration in a proportion related to the previous one. For example, a section might begin with the numbers 9/8; the meaning is not that of a grouping of nine eighths into three units of dotted quarters, but is the direction that the performer is now to sing nine notes in the time span required to sing eight of the same value, in either a previous section or as compared to another voice. Reference to the final section of the preceding example will show that the triplum is performing nine eighths to eight in the duplum and tenor; the time signature used in the original source defines this proportional relationship and is explained in a direction given by the composer as a prescription to be taken as a *canon* or rule (the original meaning of the term). This system of numerical time signatures, referred to as proportional notation, was to be fully explored by composers of the fifteenth century, but its origins lie in the late Ars Nova. With its use, rhythmic counterpoint of a highly complex nature was possible, for polyrhythmic contrasts of all kinds could be easily notated; all that was required was an understanding of some basic metric unit or combination of units which could then be further divided into smaller groups in almost limitless ways.

The artificiality of rhythmic and notational complexities seen in Chantilly is a direct reflection of the artificiality of French chivalric society during the late years of the fourteenth century. When that artificial society met its defeat in the rout at Agincourt (1415), with the slaughter of the flower of French knighthood, France fell from its high place to become the battleground for English and Burgundian expansion. Just as the kingdom so carefully built up in the days of Philip Augustus became but a shadow of its former grandeur, so did the music of its beaten society fall before the innovations of its invaders. Although certain French composers continued production, their work was quickly overshadowed by that of the new generation of English and Burgundian musicians who, like their noble masters, assumed the place of leadership.

## ITALY AT THE CLOSE OF THE ARS NOVA

Just as the close of the French Ars Nova is reflected in the Chantilly manuscript, so the final years of the Italian Trecento are summarized by two sources, one from Modena and the other, now in Paris and known as the Reina codex, from Venice. Like Chantilly, both manuscripts show the influence of French rhythmic complexity and its notation, for the same devices are used for the same purposes. Although most of the composers represented in Modena are Italian, principally from the Northern parts of that country, the major form used is that of the ballade, with stress on the use of French as the language for its texts. The madrigal, that form so typically Italian, has disappeared and the ballata is no longer of great importance.

Stylistically, the melismata no longer have the limpid flow characteristic of the music of Landini but, subject to rhythmic aberrations, have become mechanical virtuosity without musical meaning. The emphasis on rhythmic complexity has destroyed the character of vocal line that was the heart of Trecento technique in favor of an artificiality that is purely French. The line between Italian and French styles has virtually disappeared; reflecting this rapprochement, Chantilly includes twelve works also found in the Modena manuscript. As a sample of the kind of rhythmic complexity found in many of these works, Example 9-2 gives the texted uppermost line from the closing part of the ballade, "Le greygnour," by Matheus de Perusio, part of the Modena manuscript. This upper line is accompanied by two others, both of which are also filled with rhythmic complications, although not to the degree seen in the vocal line.

The major Italian survival is in the area of notation, for, although certain elements of French notational practice were early taken over by the Italians, there is still in the Modena manuscript evidence that the Italian predilection for indication of rhythmic values by unusual shapes of notes still existed. In addition to the normal French forms, there are numerous varieties of tailed notes, with flags above and below, to the right and to the left; these are placed on both full and hollow black and

EXAMPLE 9-2.

red notes, thus giving the page a strikingly exotic appearance. As in the
Chantilly manuscript, many of these notational excesses are unnecessary,
for the values could easily have been indicated in a simpler manner; there
are also many verbal directions to clarify the meaning of the notation.

Already victims of French domination, the Italians were, like the
French, destined to fall in turn before the musical talents of the *Ultra-
montani*, the men from the other side of the Alps. As early as the 1360's,
Johannes Ciconia, a native of Liège, had come to Italy as one of the first
Northerners to make his way there; although he returned to his native
land for a time, he came back to Italy again in 1403, to Padua, where he
spent the remainder of his life. While his early works show a heavy Italian
influence, those which come from the end of his life indicate the development of a newer and simpler style that was to supersede the involuted
compositions then characteristic of Italian music.

With the reestablishment of the papacy in Rome and the revival of
the chapel there, the invasion from the North led by Ciconia gradually
drove Italian musicians from places of importance. Other men from Liège,
Reims, Tournai, and, in particular, from Cambrai brought with them
a new simplicity and a new approach to harmonic sonority that was to
make of Italy a musical province of Burgundy and the Lowlands. With
their appearance, Italian music as such came to an end for a century, not
to reappear as an individual manifestation until well into the sixteenth

century. While Italy was to become supreme in the visual arts through the efforts of its native creators, in music it was to be represented during the fifteenth century by composers of almost all other parts of Europe save Italy; the history of music in Italy during the first quarter of the new century was to be represented by such musicians as Johannes Brasart, Nicholas Grenon, Guillaume Legrant, Arnold de Lantins, Johannes de Limburgia, and Guillaume Dufay, all non-Italians by both birth and musical training. To the influence of these men from Burgundy was to be added, at a slightly later date, the impact of English practice, under the leadership of John Dunstable and Leonel Power. With these two groups, the musical Renaissance properly begins.

## MUSIC THEORY AT THE CLOSE
## OF THE ARS NOVA

By the opening years of the fifteenth century, the increasingly deep cleavage between medieval speculative and practical approaches to music theory was almost complete. We have already noted the increasing tendency of theorists of the early part of the fourteenth century to concentrate their efforts upon novelties in the musical techniques of their time, the description of notational practice, improvised counterpoint and its rules, together with all other matters necessary for the education of the performer. Speculative discussion had already begun to disappear from the vast majority of these treatises as of no real importance in the study of musical technique.

At the end of the Ars Nova, this tendency had solidified into a standard procedure, particularly in view of the overpowering preoccupation of musicians with the difficulties caused by the rhythmic complications of the music then being composed. While a few speculative treatises in the medieval manner continued to be produced (those of Prosdocimus de Beldemandis, Johannes Ciconia, Anselmus of Parma, and Ugolino of Orvieto taking the major place), they all have about them an air of unreality and lack of contact with the developments of their own time. The *Nova Musica* of Ciconia, from the last years of his life, is a treatise which at first glance could easily be taken for a work of the twelfth century, for its contents make no effort to discuss in speculative terms any music composed after that date; Ciconia even speaks of organum as though it were a contemporary category, although the production of that form had long since ceased.

Some treatises attempt to fit the new developments within the old medieval framework, albeit unsuccessfully. Attempts are made, for example, to extend the Guidonian solmization system to include the new chromatics. There are efforts to suggest new ways of monochord tuning that will handle the added accidentals and give them their proper numerical ratios according to speculative procedures of the past. Finally, justifications are offered for the developments of notation, so that the same philosophical utilization can be made of these novelties as had been made of the elements of the original system. The gap between the old speculation and the new practicality, however, was far too great by this time to be successfully bridged. Ugolino's *Declaratio* is the last great effort to consider, in the medieval manner, speculation and practice as but two aspects of one great subject; after him, speculative theory was to be considered as a support for the practical, rather than vice versa. Musical practice from the fifteenth century on was to develop its rules of procedure on the basis of expediency, without need or regard for speculative niceties. During the Renaissance, when speculative justification was offered, it was to carry little weight when balanced against the sensual and affective qualities demanded by sounding music; the rules laid down by speculation would carry no obligation. Music continued to be taught in Renaissance universities as a speculative subject, but the raw material of its study was no longer tied, as it had been in the Middle Ages, to contemporary practice; its flavor was antiquarian and its meaning not immediate.

## CONCLUSION

Music in the Middle Ages, like all the arts, had its required function, one without which it could not have existed. This function, a double one as a stage of the *quadrivium* and as a part of medieval ecclesiastical rites, gave it an impetus toward development and complication that led it to the heights of the thirteenth century. Spurred on by the twin demands of the philosopher and the Church, musicians bent their energies to furnishing music that could satisfy to the fullest extent the needs of both. As a necessary part of education, music became an integral part of that way of thinking that still remains as a monument to the mental capabilities of medieval man. As a servant of the organizing leadership of the Middle Ages, the Church, music could and did develop its potentialities in perfect balance with the functions required of it therein. No greater fulfillment of both an aesthetic and a practical pair of goals can be found than in the music of Leonin and Perotin, where the services of the Church stand enhanced with that *musica instrumentalis* which implies within its sounding structures the superior *musica humana* and *musica mundana*.

Yet, as always, within the full flowering of perfection the seeds of decay were contained. With the passing of the thirteenth century, the failure of the Church to maintain its supremacy as the guide of the world and center of human existence led to a degradation of its function and a disregard for its needs that eventually gave free rein to the practicing musicians' interest in the intricacies of technique for its own sake, with the exaltation of the purely sensual. No longer under firm control, excessive interest in goals and procedures not tied to the earlier central purposes of music gave a centrifugal force to its concrete manifestations so great that disintegration could be the only result. With no meaning except that of technical intricacy, the music of the late Ars Nova could only vanish with the appearance of a new age, one with new and clear aesthetic goals and functions within which musicians could now find a secure place. This new age we call the Renaissance.

## BIBLIOGRAPHICAL NOTES

For the secular music of the period covered in this chapter, two collections cited in the bibliographical notes of Chapter 7, Apel's *French Secular Compositions of the Fourteenth Century* and Wilkins's *A 14th Century Repertory from the Codex Reina*, are major sources. Apel has published a second, smaller collection, *French Secular Music of the Late Fourteenth Century* (Cambridge: Mediaeval Academy, 1950); its introduction is a thorough survey of all facets of the problems, while the musical portion includes representative compositions in all categories. The book also includes ten facsimiles of works from Chantilly, Modena, etc., graphically demonstrating the ornate character of the music. Nigel E. Wilkins's *A 15th-Century Repertory from the Codex Reina* (Rome: American Institute of Musicology, 1964) is a sequel to the fourteenth-century material from this codex mentioned above. For the motets from the major sources, see Ursula Günther, *The Motets of the Manuscripts Chantilly . . . and Modena . . .* (Rome: American Institute of Musicology, 1965). Music from the turn of the century is contained in Gilbert Reaney, *Early Fifteenth Century Music* (Rome, American Institute of Musicology, 1955– ); this is a continuing series of which five volumes have appeared. Both French and Italian composers are represented in this collection. Other works may be found in Gaetano Cesari and Fabio Fano, *La Cappella Musicale del Duomo di Milano* (Milano: Ricordi, 1956). The complete works of Johannes Ciconia appear as the second volume of Suzanne Clercx-Lejeune, *Johannes Ciconia* (Bruxelles: Palais des Académies, 1960); the first volume is the definitive study of this composer.

The various articles by Gilbert Reaney, Leonard Ellinwood, Frank Ll. Harrison, Manfred Bukofzer, and Rudolf von Ficker in the *New Oxford History of Music*, III, are excellent summaries; their various bibliog-

raphies, though mainly of works not in English, are quite valuable. Kurt
von Fischer has given a thorough study of the Reina Codex in *Musica
Disciplina*, XI (1957); a similar study of the Chantilly manuscript by
Gilbert Reaney appears in the same journal, VIII (1954) and X (1956).

# INDEX